(Continued)

Young Children
Continue to
Reinvent Arithmetic
— 2nd Grade —

IMPLICATIONS OF PIAGET'S THEORY

SECOND EDITION

Constance Kamii
with Linda Leslie Joseph

Teachers College, Columbia University
New York and London

Published by Teachers College Press, 1234 Amsterdam Avenue, New York, NY 10027

Copyright © 2004 by Teachers College, Columbia University

Library of Congress Cataloging-in-Publication Data

Kamii, Constance.
    Young children continue to reinvent arithmetic—2nd grade : implications of
Piaget's theory / Constance Kamii with Linda Leslie Joseph.—2nd ed.
      p.   cm.—(Early childhood education series)
    Includes bibliographical references and index.
    ISBN 0-8077-4404-2 (cloth : alk. paper)—ISBN 0-8077-4403-4 (pbk. : alk. paper)
    1. Arithmetic—Study and teaching (Elementary)   2. Number concept—Study and
teaching (Elementary)   3. Piaget, Jean, 1896-   I. Joseph, Linda Leslie.   II. Title.
III. Early childhood education series (Teachers College Press)

QA135.6.K36 2003
372.7—dc21   2003050765

ISBN 0-8077-4403-4 (paper)
ISBN 0-8077-4404-2 (cloth)

Printed on acid-free paper
Manufactured in the United States of America

11 10 09 08 07 06 05 04   8 7 6 5 4 3 2 1

Contents

Introduction to the Second Edition

WE HAVE FELT the need to revise the first edition of this book since we became aware of the harmful effects of teaching "carrying" and "borrowing" to second graders. When we wrote the first edition in 1988, we had no idea that this teaching was harmful to children. We thought that our students, who invented their own procedures for multidigit addition and subtraction, were just doing better than those receiving traditional instruction.

By 1990, however, we had begun to think that many children invented illogical computational rules (often called "buggy algorithms") because they could not make sense of "carrying" and "borrowing." Research by Ashlock (1972, 1976, 1982, 1986) and Brown and Burton (1978) in the United States; Plunkett (1979) in England; Carraher, Carraher, and Schliemann (1985; Carraher & Schliemann, 1985) in Brazil; and many others converged toward the hypothesis that the teaching of conventional algorithms was harming children. We confirmed this hypothesis by 1992, as can be seen in *Young Children Continue to Reinvent Arithmetic, 3rd Grade* (Kamii, 1994). Since then, we have felt the need to revise our book about second grade to make this important point. Chapter 2 of the present volume explains why these algorithms are harmful.

Other factors also motivated this revision. First, the research we recently conducted on subtraction (Kamii, Lewis, & Kirkland, 2001) led us to understand why subtraction is much harder than addition, and why it should be de-emphasized until knowledge of sums becomes solid. We also learned that multidigit subtraction with regrouping is hard even for some fourth and fifth graders.

Other studies we conducted in the 1990s enabled us to understand the difference between repeated addition and multiplication (Clark & Kamii, 1996). We also learned that kindergartners can solve simple multiplication and division word problems (Carpenter, Ansell, Franke, Fennema, & Weisbeck, 1993). Young children use repeated addition to solve these problems that we thought had to be solved with multiplication and division. These points are discussed in Chapter 5 of the present volume, along with principles of teaching in Chapter 6, which are conceptualized more tightly than before.

Since 1988, mathematics education has progressed in some ways and regressed in other ways. On the side of progress is the fact that countless researchers and teachers all over the United States and abroad are now encouraging children to invent their own procedures instead of using textbooks and workbooks (Carpenter, Fennema, Franke, Levi, & Empson, 1999; Economopoulos & Russell, 1998; Fosnot & Dolk, 2001; Hiebert et al., 1997; Richardson, 1999; Shifter, Bastable, & Russell, 1999; Trafton & Thiessen, 1999; Yackel, Cobb, Wood, Wheatley, & Merkel, 1990). When Linda Joseph and I began to work together in 1984, we thought we were the only ones in the country trying to encourage children to invent their own procedures. The fact that many teachers and researchers have changed in the same way so quickly foreshadows the progress that can be expected in the future.

On the other hand, testmania and "drill and kill" have become worse since 1988, and "math wars" have appeared. It is truly regrettable that so much money and human effort have to be wasted on "quick fixes." When testmania is proven to have failed, the way will be open to those who have studied how children learn mathematics. Force-feeding children and coercing educators to attain statistically impossible goals can result only in failure.

Linda Joseph was an outstanding teacher when we wrote the first edition of this book, and she is now the principal of an elementary school. While testmania and "quick fixes" are dominating the surface of education today, Linda's rise to a leadership position is a sign of a strong constructivist undercurrent that sooner or later will emerge as the dominant force. If educators base their practice on a scientific explanation of how children learn mathematics, constructivist teaching will continue to grow. Science does not swing back and forth like the old pendulum that characterizes education, and constructivist teaching is likely to keep advancing toward wider acceptance.

PART I

Theoretical Foundation

CHAPTER 1

Why Advocate Children's Reinventing Arithmetic?

WHY DO WE WANT children to reinvent arithmetic, when we can simply tell them how to add, subtract, multiply, and divide? The answer to this question is presented in this chapter and developed throughout this book. We will begin with the epistemological background behind Piaget's constructivism to show that his thinking was fundamentally different from the empiricist, commonsense assumptions on which education has been based for centuries. According to common sense, human beings acquire knowledge by *internalizing* it from the environment. Piaget showed with scientific evidence, however, that each child *constructs*, or *creates*, logico-mathematical knowledge from within.

The conservation of number will be discussed as an example proving that children all over the world construct number concepts through their own logical thinking, without any instruction. The chapter will conclude with the importance of basing teaching on a scientific theory that explains how children *construct* arithmetic. It is time for educators to stop teaching on the basis of mere tradition, fashions, personal philosophies, and outdated science.

PIAGET'S CONSTRUCTIVISM IN THE HISTORY OF EPISTEMOLOGY

Piaget often is believed to have been a psychologist, but he was actually an epistemologist. Epistemology is the study of knowledge that addresses questions like "How do we know what we think we know?" and "How can we know whether or not what we think we know is true?"

Since the time before the Greeks, two main currents have developed in response to these questions: empiricism and rationalism. Empiricists (such as Locke, Berkeley, and Hume) argued in essence that the source of knowledge is outside the individual and that knowledge is acquired by *internalization* through the senses. Empiricists further argued that a baby's

3

mind is like a clean slate, and experiences are "written" on this slate as the child grows older. Locke (1690/1947) is especially well known for having said, "The senses at first let in particular ideas, and furnish the yet empty cabinet, and the mind by degrees growing familiar with some of them, they are lodged in the memory" (p. 22).

Rationalists (such as Descartes, Spinoza, and Kant) did not deny the importance of sensory experience, but they argued that *reason* is more important and powerful than sensory information. They pointed out, for example, that since our senses *deceive* us in perceptual illusions, sensory experiences cannot be trusted to give us truth with certitude. The rigor, precision, and certainty of mathematics were the rationalists' best proof of the power of reason. Another example they gave was our knowledge that every event has a cause, even though we cannot examine every event in all the past and future of the universe. When rationalists had to explain the origin of this power of reason, some of them said that certain kinds of knowledge or concepts are innate and unfold as the individual matures.

Piaget saw elements of truth and untruth in both traditions. As a scientist trained in biology, he refused to continue the debate based on philosophical speculation. The only way to resolve the epistemological conflict, he said, was to study the origin and development of knowledge scientifically. With this conviction, he wanted to study humanity's construction of mathematics and science from its prehistoric beginnings because he believed that, to understand human knowledge, it was necessary to study its origin and development rather than only the end product. However, the prehistoric and historical evidence was no longer available, and this is why he decided to study the development of empirical knowledge and reason in children. His study of children was thus a means to answer epistemological questions scientifically.

While Piaget saw the importance both of sensory information and of reason, he aligned himself with rationalists when he had to categorize himself. His 60 years of research with children was motivated to a large extent by a desire to prove the inadequacy of empiricism. The well-known conservation tasks must be understood in this context. To clarify this statement, it is necessary to discuss the three kinds of knowledge Piaget distinguished.

THE NATURE OF LOGICO-MATHEMATICAL KNOWLEDGE

The Three Kinds of Knowledge

Piaget (1967/1971; see also Piaget, 1945/1951) identified three kinds of knowledge according to their ultimate sources and modes of structuring—physical knowledge, social-conventional knowledge, and logico-mathematical knowledge.

Physical knowledge is knowledge of objects in the external world. Our knowledge of the color and weight of counters or any other object is an example of physical knowledge. The ultimate source of physical knowledge is partly *in* objects, and physical knowledge can be acquired empirically through experience and observation. (Our reason for saying "partly" will be explained in Chapter 2.)

Examples of *social-conventional knowledge* are words such as "one–two–three" and "uno–dos–tres," which were created by convention among people. Other examples of social-conventional knowledge are standard units of measurement such as inches and centimeters and social rules like "ladies first." The ultimate source of social knowledge is partly in conventions made by people, and social transmission is necessary for children's acquisition of social knowledge. (Our reason for saying "partly" also will be clarified in Chapter 2.)

Logico-mathematical knowledge consists of mental relationships, and the ultimate source of these relationships is each individual's mind. For instance, when we see a red counter and a blue one, we can think about them as being *different, similar,* or *two.* If we focus on their colors, the counters are different. If we ignore colors, the counters are similar, and if we think about them numerically, the counters become two.

("Two" is not a good number to choose to illustrate the logico-mathematical nature of number concepts because two is a small, *perceptual* number. Small numbers up to four or five are perceptual numbers that can be distinguised at a glance even by some birds. However, "two" also can be a *logico-mathematical* number. We chose the number "two" because, with two objects, we could illustrate other mental relationships such as "similar" and "different.")

Children construct logico-mathematical knowledge by putting previously made relationships into new relationships. For example, by coordinating the relationships of "same" and "different" that they initially created between two objects, children go on to make classes and subclasses (Inhelder & Piaget, 1959/1964). When they can make classes and subclasses, they become able to deduce logically that there are more animals in the world than dogs, without empirically counting all the animals in the world. Likewise, by putting 4 twos into relationships, they become able to deduce that $2 + 2 + 2 + 2 = 8$, that $4 \times 2 = 8$, and that if $4x = 8$, x must be 2.

Piaget thus recognized external and internal sources of knowledge. The source of physical and social knowledge is partly external to the individual, but the source of logico-mathematical knowledge is internal. This statement will be clarified in Chapter 2, when we discuss the two kinds of abstraction distinguished by Piaget. Let us review the conservation-of-number task, which will clarify the difference between empirical, physical knowledge and logico-mathematical knowledge.

The Conservation-of-Number Task

In this task (Inhelder, Sinclair, & Bovet, 1974; Piaget & Szeminska, 1941/1965), the interviewer first makes a line of eight red counters. Offering about 20 blue counters to the child, the interviewer then asks him or her to put out "the same number" (or "the same much" or "just as many"). (Eight objects are usually used because it is not possible to differentiate between "ooooooo" and "oooooooo," for example, perceptually.)

If the child puts out the same number of counters with one-to-one correspondence, the interviewer says, "Watch what I'm going to do," and pushes one row of counters close together and spreads out the other row (see Figure 1.1). The question then asked is, "Are there as many counters here as here [running a finger along each row], or are there more here [indicating one row] or more here [indicating the other row]?" The question then asked is, "How do you know?"

Nonconservers think that there are more in one row, usually the longer one, than in the other. Conservers, on the other hand, reply that there are just as many red ones as blue ones and give one of the following three logical explanations:

- "You didn't add or take anything away" (the *identity* argument).
- "We could put all the red ones back to the way they were, and you'll see that there's the same number" (the *reversibility* argument).
- "The red line is longer, but there's more space in between. So the number is still the same" (the *compensation* argument).

The conservation task is thus a test of children's logico-mathematical knowledge. The knowledge that counters stay on the table without melting like ice cubes is physical knowledge. However, the ability to deduce logically that the quantity in the two rows has to be the same is logico-mathematical knowledge. Only when children can make numerical relationships among the counters, can they reason, with *the force of logical necessity*, that the two rows have the same number.

Number: The Synthesis of Hierarchical Inclusion and Order. Piaget went on to explain that children construct number concepts by synthesizing two kinds of mental relationships—hierarchical inclusion and order.

Figure 1.1. The arrangement of the counters when the question is asked about conservation.

Hierarchical Inclusion. Hierarchical inclusion refers to the child's ability to mentally include "one" in "two," "two" in "three," "three" in "four," and so on. If we ask 4-year-olds to count eight objects arranged in a row, they often count them correctly and announce that there are "eight." If we then ask them to "show me eight," they often point to the eighth object, saying, "That one," as shown in Figure 1.2(a). This behavior indicates that, for these children, the words *one, two, three,* and so on, are names for individual elements in a series, like *Monday, Tuesday, Wednesday,* and so forth (social-conventional knowledge). For these children, the word *eight* stands for the last object in the series and not for the entire group.

To quantify a collection of objects numerically (logico-mathematical knowledge), a child has to put them into a relationship of hierarchical inclusion, as shown in Figure 1.2(b). When presented with eight objects,

Figure 1.2. The (a) absence and (b) presence of hierarchical inclusion in a child's mind.

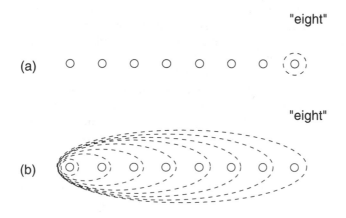

the child can quantify the collection numerically only if he or she can mentally include "one" in "two," "two" in "three," and so on.

Four-year-olds' reaction to the class-inclusion task helps us understand how difficult it is for young children to make a hierarchical structure (Inhelder & Piaget, 1959/1964). In the class-inclusion task, the child is presented with six counters—four blue ones and two red ones, for example. He or she first is asked, "What shall we call these?" so that the interviewer can use words from the child's vocabulary. The child then is asked to show "*all* the circles," "*all* the blue circles," and "*all* the red circles," using the words he or she used. Only after ascertaining the child's understanding of these words does the adult ask the following class-inclusion question: "Are there more blue circles or more circles?"

Four-year-olds typically answer, "More blue ones," whereupon the adult asks, "Than what?" The 4-year-old's usual answer is, "Than red ones." In other words, the interviewer asks, "Are there more blue circles or more circles?" but young children "hear" this question as, "Are there more blue circles or more red ones?" Young children hear a question that is different from the one the adult asks because once they mentally cut the whole (circles) into two parts (blue circles and red circles), the only thing they can think about is the two parts. For them at that moment, the whole does not exist any more. They can think about the whole, but not when they are thinking about the parts. To compare the whole with a part, the child has to perform two opposite mental actions *at the same time*—cut the whole into two parts and put the parts back together into a whole. This is precisely what 4-year-olds cannot do.

By 7 to 8 years of age, most children's thought becomes mobile enough to be reversible. Reversibility refers to the ability to mentally perform two opposite actions *simultaneously*—in this case, cutting the whole into two parts and putting the parts back into a whole. In physical action, it is impossible to do two opposite things simultaneously. In our minds, however, this is possible when thought has become mobile enough to be reversible. Only when the parts can be reunited in the mind, can a child "see" that there are more circles than blue circles.

The class-inclusion task proves the inadequacy of empiricism. All the circles remain in front of the 4-year-old, but 4-year-olds cannot *see* these "circles" when they cannot *think about* them. They can see the "circles," "the blue ones," and "red ones," one group at a time, but they cannot *see* the total group and a subgroup at the same time because they cannot think about them at the same time.

Order. Order refers to the child's ability to mentally arrange a set of objects into "first," "second," "third," and so on. All teachers of young children have seen the common tendency among 4-year-olds to count objects by skipping some and counting others more than once. When given 10 objects arranged randomly, a child who can recite "one, two, three, four . . ." up to 30 (social-conventional knowledge) may count the same objects more than once and claim that there are 30. This behavior shows that the child does not feel the *logical necessity* (logico-mathematical knowledge) of putting the objects into a relationship of order to make sure not to skip any or count the same object(s) more than once. The only way we can be sure of not overlooking any or counting the same object more than once is by putting them into a relationship of order. It is not necessary for the child to put the objects in a spatial order. What is important is that he or she order them *mentally*.

Why Do Conservers Conserve and Nonconservers Do Not? Conservation can now be explained by the mental structure of number that children gradually construct. This structure (logico-mathematical knowledge) results from the synthesis of hierarchical inclusion and order, as discussed above. Conservers conserve because they have constructed this logico-mathematical knowledge. Nonconservers do not conserve because their logico-mathematical knowledge is not yet strong enough to overcome the empirical appearance of the two rows.

The reader must have noted that children conserve or do not conserve by doing their own thinking. However, most authors of books about Piaget's theory misinterpret conservation by assimilating Piaget's theory to their empiricist thinking. For example, Ginsburg and Opper (1988) say that nonconservers "fail to understand" conservation, and that they fail "to appreciate certain basic constancies or invariants in the environment" (p. 141). Conservation is not "out there" for children to understand or appreciate. Conservation is a *logical deduction*, which takes place in each child's head.

Many other authors tell us that children "discover" and "recognize" conservation. These terms also reflect an empiricist misunderstanding of Piaget's theory. As Piaget pointed out, America was already "out there" when it was discovered, but the automobile was not. The automobile was *invented* because it was not "out there" to be discovered. When we say that young children invent arithmetic, we clearly mean that children invent their own arithmetic rather than discovering it.

The Universality of Logico-Mathematical Knowledge

Cross-cultural studies in Aden (Hyde, 1959), Algeria (Bovet, 1974), Iran (Mohseni, 1966), Martinique (Piaget, 1966), Nigeria (Price-Williams, 1961),

Montreal and Rwanda (Laurendeau-Bendavid, 1977), Scotland and Ghana (Adjei, 1977), and Thailand (Opper, 1977) are among the investigations giving evidence that children all over the world become able to conserve continuous and discontinuous quantities (number as well as amounts of liquid and clay). Children of indigenous peoples such as the Aborigines in Australia (Dasen, 1974; De Lemos, 1969) and the Atayal in Taiwan (Kohlberg, 1968) also have been found to conserve without any instruction.

The ages of attainment vary from one group to another, but the fact of this attainment remains certain. Researchers who have studied deaf children (Furth, 1966), blind children (Hatwell, 1966), and children and adolescents with severe mental retardation (Inhelder, 1943/1968) also have reported that these children attain the conservation of continuous and discontinuous quantities. Logico-mathematical knowledge is thus universal, and 2 and 2 make 4 in every country.

Why do we want children to invent arithmetic when we can simply show them how to add and subtract? Based on empiricist assumptions, educators have believed for centuries that, without instruction, children were incapable of adding or subtracting numbers. After all, if they were clean slates or empty containers at birth, knowledge had to be supplied from the outside. On the basis of Piaget's research and revolutionary theory and its cross-cultural verification, however, I hypothesized in 1980 that if children construct their own number concepts, they should be able to invent arithmetic for themselves, without instruction. If 5, for example, is (1 + 1 + 1 + 1 + 1), which children invent, 5 + 3 is (1 + 1 + 1 + 1 + 1) + (1 + 1 + 1), which should be equally inventable. This hypothesis was amply verified in 1980–81 and 1981–82 by Georgia DeClark's first graders (Kamii, 1985). It continues to be verified every year in an increasingly large number of classrooms in the United States (Kamii, 2000) and abroad.

In second grade, there is another important reason for encouraging children to invent their own arithmetic: Second-grade arithmetic includes multidigit addition and subtraction, and the teaching of "carrying" and "borrowing" has been found to be harmful, as will be explained in Chapter 2. We thus advocate second graders' invention of second-grade arithmetic not only because they can invent it but also because this invention protects them from the harm caused by the teaching of "carrying" and "borrowing."

THE IMPORTANCE OF A SCIENTIFIC, EXPLANATORY THEORY

Principles and Standards for School Mathematics (National Council of Teachers of Mathematics, 2000) represents enormous progress in mathematics education, and most of its authors were generally sympathetic to constructivism. However, their thinking was still diffuse and empiricist, as can be seen in statements such as, "Understanding of number develops in prekindergarten through grade 2 as children count and learn to recognize 'how many' in sets of objects" (p. 33). Children *construct* number from the inside, rather than learning to "recognize" it as if number were "out there" to be *recognized* empirically.

The preceding paragraph may seem like academic hairsplitting, but it illustrates how educators do not base principles of teaching on a rigorous scientific theory that *explains how children learn*. The lack of a scientific, explanatory theory keeps education vulnerable to fads, "math wars," and the swinging of the pendulum for which education is famous.

Medicine has a solid scientific base, and there is no disagreement, for example, about the fact that the cause of cancer has not been explained scientifically. Disagreement about how to treat cancer always begins with agreement about what is known and unknown scientifically about its cause(s). In medicine, there is no swinging of the pendulum back and forth because science does not go back to yesterday's truth.

The heliocentric theory took 150 years to be universally accepted (Taylor, 1949), but once humanity accepted it, we have never gone back to the geocentric theory. Strictly speaking, the business of science is only to *describe* and *explain* phenomena. The practical application of an explanatory theory to applied fields like medicine, navigation, architecture, and education is not the concern of science itself. However, a scientific theory can be enormously useful in an applied field because it enables us to *focus the debate* on *how children learn* arithmetic (or any other subject) rather than on the effectiveness of "this method" versus "that method" of teaching.

Many people in education and politics are now insisting on basing decisions about teaching on "scientific evidence." These people are merely comparing the effectiveness of "this method" versus "that method," without any awareness that many data are based on old, outdated, empiricist science. Such comparisons can lead only to contradictory findings because each camp has different goals and objectives and collects different kinds of data that it considers to be valid. Examples of glaringly contradictory findings can be found in Chapter 10 of this book. It also will be pointed out in Chapter 10 that achievement tests do not assess second graders on estimation, mental arithmetic, or the logic involved in word problems. Multiple-choice tests can tap only superficial, surface bits of knowledge. Because different data are based on different assumptions about the nature of knowledge, contradictory "evidence" is inevitable, and "math wars" can be expected to continue for many years to come.

The nature of scientific revolutions was elucidated by Kuhn (1970), who pointed out that scientists' first reaction to a revolutionary theory is resistance. The acceptance of a new, revolutionary theory takes time, he said with many examples, because truth is a social phenomenon. A truth requires consensus to be accepted as a scientific truth, and it takes time even for scientists to give up their vested interest in their old ways of thinking. The heliocentric theory, revolutionary in the sixteenth and seventeenth centuries, took 150 years to become universally accepted also because of the resistance of the Church. Today, the powerful institutions supporting old, empiricist beliefs in drill and practice are political and economic. Politicians are passing laws in the name of "accountability," and businesspeople are strongly supporting these laws. For some businesses, furthermore, these laws mean enormous profits from the sale of tests, aligned textbooks, test-preparation materials, and services.

However, increasing numbers of teachers, principals, teacher educators, curriculum developers, and researchers are now advocating constructivist teaching. When Linda Joseph and I began to work together in 1984, we thought we were the only educators in the country advocating children's invention of their own procedures for multidigit addition and subtraction. Today, only 19 year later, however, there are countless teachers and others in America and abroad who are no longer using textbooks and workbooks and are, instead, encouraging children to do their own thinking. Once having seen children's creativity, confidence, and pride in their own ability to think, teachers cannot go back to the deadly worksheets they previously used to teach "carrying" and "borrowing." We are totally confident that we will win the "math wars" in the long run.

CHAPTER 2

Place Value: How Is It Learned and Unlearned?

"PLACE VALUE" REFERS to the social-conventional knowledge that in "333," for example, the first 3 means three hundred (or 3 hundreds), the second 3 means thirty (or 3 tens), and the third 3 means three (or 3 ones). Place value is now taught in first grade, and again in every subsequent grade of elementary school. Research has shown, however, that most children think that the "1" in "16" means *one* until about fourth grade. These findings were first reported by Mieko Kamii (1980, 1982) and later confirmed by other researchers such as Ross (1986). In this chapter, we will review her study and Cauley's (1988), explain the nature of representation and how place value is learned, and discuss how the algorithms of "carrying" and "borrowing" "unteach" place value.

CHILDREN'S POOR KNOWLEDGE OF PLACE VALUE

Ross's Study

Ross (1986) built on Mieko Kamii's (1980, 1982) work, as well as that of Resnick (1982, 1983) and others, in a comprehensive study of children's knowledge of place value. The subjects in her study consisted of 60 children, 15 each in grades 2 through 5. Her sampling was unusual in that she randomly selected children from 33 classrooms "from the grade level enrollment lists of five elementary schools in Butte County, California. . . . The schools were selected to represent urban and rural communities, public and private funding, and diversity with respect to the mathematics textbook series used, school size, and social class" (p. 3).

In one of her tasks, Ross presented 25 tongue depressors to each child, in individual interviews, and asked him or her to count them and to "write down the number." She then circled the 5 of 25 and asked, "Does this part have anything to do with how many sticks you have?"

13

After the child's response, she circled the 2 and asked the same question about its meaning.

The four levels of response she found were the following:

Level 1. The child thinks that "25" stands for the whole numerical quantity, but that the individual digits have no numerical meaning.

Level 2. The child thinks that "25" stands for the whole numerical quantity but *invents* numerical meanings for the individual digits. For example, the child thinks the "5" means groups of 5 sticks, and the "2" means groups of 2 sticks.

Level 3. The child thinks that "25" stands for the whole numerical quantity and that the individual digits have meanings related to groups of tens or ones but has only a partial or confused idea of how this all works. The sum of the parts need not equal the whole. For example, the child thinks that both individual digits mean ones, or that "5" stands for tens and "2" stands for ones.

Level 4. The child thinks that "25" stands for the whole numerical quantity, that the "5" stands for ones, that the "2" stands for tens, and that the whole must equal the sum of the parts (Ross, 1986, p. 5).

As can be seen in Table 2.1 and the following statement, Ross found essentially the same thing as did Mieko Kamii (1980, 1982): "While every child in the study was able to determine the number of sticks and write the appropriate numeral, not until grade 4 did half the children demon-

Table 2.1: Performance on Sticks Task (by number of children)

	Level of Performance			
Grade	1	2	3	4
2	5	2	5	3
3	7	1	2	5
4	0	7	0	8
5	1	4	0	10
Total	13	14	7	26

$n = 15$ for each grade

chi-square $= 30.1$; $df = 9$; $p < .0004$

From *The Development of Children's Place-Value Numeration Concepts in Grades Two through Five,* by S. H. Ross, 1986, paper presented at the annual meeting of the American Educational Research Association, San Francisco, p. 6. Reprinted with permission.

strate that they knew that the 5 represented five sticks and the 2 represented 20 sticks" (p. 5).

Cauley's Study

The study by Cauley (1988) is different from the preceding one in that it involved subtraction and revealed children's inability to understand place value while being able to produce correct answers. In a suburban public school and an urban Catholic school in Delaware, Cauley identified 34 of 90 second and third graders as being proficient in "borrowing." She interviewed the 34 students individually, and they produced correct answers, as shown in Figure 2.1. One of the questions she then asked was: "Before you borrowed you had [56] and after you borrowed you had this much [circling the 56 and all the borrowing marks]; did you have more before you borrowed, or after you borrowed, or was it the same?" (p. 203).

Only 41% of the 34 students replied that the number was the same after borrowing. Thirty-two percent said they had more before borrowing (because, for example, 5 is more than 4), and 24% said they had more after borrowing (because, for example, 16 is more than 6). As the 34 students comprised about a third of the 90 students, the proportion of all second and third graders who said the 56 remained the same was about 14%.

HOW IS PLACE VALUE LEARNED?

Mathematics educators generally do not differentiate between abstraction and representation and think that the use of concrete objects automatically makes an activity concrete, and that an activity is necessarily abstract if it involves written numerals. However, Piaget made a clear distinction between abstraction and representation and pointed out that children can

Figure 2.1. Children's written work in Cauley's study of subtraction with "borrowing."

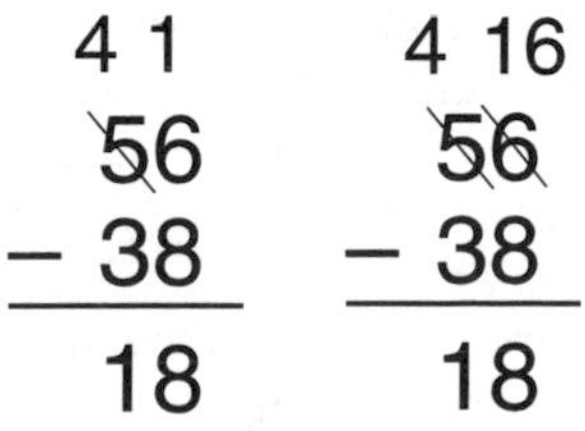

use concrete objects at a high or low level of abstraction, and that they can use written symbols at a high or low level of abstraction. This theory enables us to understand that, in Ross's study, the children who said that the 2 in 25 meant "twenty" said so because they were at a higher level of abstraction than those who said that it meant "two." Let us discuss Piaget's theory of abstraction to clarify what he meant.

Piaget's Theory of Abstraction

Piaget (1978) made a distinction between two kinds of abstraction: *empirical* abstraction and *constructive* abstraction. In *empirical abstraction*, we focus on a certain property of the object and ignore other properties. For example, when we abstract the color of an object, we focus on color and ignore all other properties such as weight and the material of which the object is made (plastic, for instance).

Constructive abstraction involves the making of mental relationships between and among objects, such as "similar," "different," and "two." As stated in Chapter 1, these relationships do not have an existence in the external world. The similarity or difference between one counter and another is constructed, or mentally made, by each individual by constructive abstraction.

Constructive abstraction also is known as "reflective" or "reflecting" abstraction. The French term Piaget usually used was *abstraction réfléchissante*, which has been translated as "reflective" or "reflecting" abstraction. Piaget occasionally used the term *constructive* abstraction, which seems easier to understand. By now readers must have inferred, correctly, that logico-mathematical knowledge is constructed by constructive abstraction and empirical abstraction is involved in the construction of physical knowledge.

The conservation-of-number task demonstrates that concrete objects can be used at a high or low level of abstraction. Nonconserving children cannot conserve because their thinking is at a low level of constructive abstraction. They have the physical knowledge of the objects in the two rows but not the logico-mathematical knowledge of number. When these children reach a higher level of constructive abstraction, they begin to conserve the numerical equivalence.

Having made the theoretical distinction between empirical and constructive abstraction, Piaget went on to say that, in the psychological reality of the young child, one kind of abstraction cannot take place without the other. For example, it would be impossible for children to make the relationship "different" or "similar" (logico-mathematical knowledge) if there were no objects in their world that are different or similar (physical knowledge). Conversely, the child could not see that a counter is red (physical knowledge) without making the category of "color" (logico-mathematical knowledge) that enables him or her to focus on color as opposed to all other properties, such as weight. Logico-mathematical knowledge (built by constructive abstraction) is thus necessary for empirical abstraction because children could not "read" facts from external reality if each fact were an isolated bit of knowledge, with no relationship to the knowledge already built and organized. This is why we said in Chapter 1 that the source of physical knowledge is only *partly* in objects and that the source of social knowledge is only *partly* in conventions made by people.

While constructive abstraction cannot take place independently of empirical abstraction up to about age 6, constructive abstraction gradually becomes independent after this age. For example, after the child has constructed number (by constructive abstraction), he or she becomes able to operate on numbers and do 5 + 5 + 5 + 5 and 4 × 5 without empirical abstraction from objects. Arithmetic and algebra are constructed by each child by making higher-level relationships out of the lower-level relationships created before.

Piaget's Theory of Representation

In empiricist thinking, it is correct to say that the symbol "+" represents addition, that the "2" in "23" represents "twenty," and that base-ten blocks represent the base-ten system. In Piaget's theory, however, all the previous statements are incorrect because representation is what a human being does. Symbols do not represent; it is always a human being who uses a symbol to represent an idea. Therefore, a human being at a low level of constructive abstraction uses symbols at a low level of abstraction. When that person reaches a higher level of constructive abstraction, he or she begins to use the same symbols at a higher level.

In Chapter 1, we saw the example of 4-year-olds who count eight objects correctly and announce that there are "eight." When asked to "show me eight," however, these children often point to the eighth object. Hierarchical inclusion of "one" in "two," "two" in "three," and so on, is achieved by constructive abstraction, and children who cannot make these mental relationships can think only about one object at a time. This is why, for them, "one" means the first object, "two" means the second object, and "eight" means the eighth object. The 4-year-olds who "count" by skipping some objects and counting others more than once likewise are using spoken numerals (social-conventional knowledge) at their low level of abstraction (logico-mathematical knowledge). When they feel the logical necessity of putting the objects into a relationship of order, they begin to count every object once and only once.

Children also represent numerical quantities by drawing pictures and writing numerals. Kato, Kamii, Ozaki, and Nagahiro (2002) showed small groups of objects (such as four dishes, six pencils, and eight small blocks) to 4- to 7-year-olds in Japan and asked them to draw/write "what's here on this sheet of paper so that your mother will be able to tell what I showed you." (In spoken Japanese, the words for "draw" and "write" sound exactly the same.) The children clearly demonstrated a close relationship between their levels of abstraction and of representation.

Those who could not make a one-to-one correspondence in the conservation task (thereby showing a low level of constructive abstraction) drew an incorrect number of objects. By contrast, most of those who could make a one-to-one correspondence in the conservation task drew the correct number of objects. Numerals were used only by conservers. An interesting finding was that 42% of those who knew how to write numerals drew pictures, revealing their preference for representing each object in the set rather than the total quantity with one numeral.

Ross (1986) gave another task using base-ten blocks to the same 60 children described earlier. She gave 40 unit blocks, several long blocks (tens), and some flat ones (hundreds) to each child and asked him or her to "use these counting blocks to build 52." Nine of the 15 second graders (60%) and most of the older students used five long blocks and two unit blocks to represent 52. If the child was successful in making 52, Ross went on to ask, "Can you find another way to represent 52?" Of the 15 students at each grade level, only 2 (13%), 8 (53%), 9 (60%), and 11 (73%), in grades 2–5, respectively, changed their initial representation to 4 ten blocks and 12 unit blocks. Only for 13% of the second graders was "ten *ones*" the same thing as "one *ten*."

Ross's two studies, Cauley's research, as well as that of Kato and colleagues demonstrate that representation is what people do at their respective levels of abstraction. Children who are at a high level of abstraction use objects (such as base-ten blocks), pictures, and numerals to represent numerical ideas at a high level of abstraction. Those who are at a low level of abstraction use the same objects, pictures, and numerals to represent numerical ideas at a low level of abstraction.

The Logico-Mathematical Knowledge of Tens and Ones

Figure 2.2(a) shows how kindergartners and most first graders think when they think "thirty-four." For them, 34 is 34 *ones*, which they constructed through constructive abstraction. Figure 2.2(b) shows how adults and older children think when they think "thirty-four." For us, 34 is 3 *tens* and 4 *ones*. What is important to note in Figure 2.2(b) is that adults and older

Figure 2.2. The structure of (a) 34 *ones* and (b) 3 *tens* and 4 *ones*.

(a) Thirty-four ones

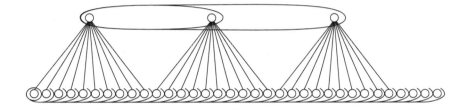

(b) Three tens and four ones

children think "one *ten*" and "ten *ones*" *simultaneously*. Many second graders can think "one *ten*" and "ten *ones*" at two different times but not at the same time. Another task devised by Ross (1986) demonstrates the difference between young children's thinking about *tens* and *ones* at two different times and older children's simultaneous thinking.

In individual interviews, Ross presented many lima beans and 9 one-ounce plastic cups to the same 60 children described earlier and asked them to put 10 beans into each cup. When a child had four cupfuls (each containing 10 beans) and eight loose ones, Ross asked, "How many beans do you think there are here altogether?" She found the following three levels:

Level 1. The children were simply unable to count the beans.
Level 2. The children counted the beans mostly by ones, rather than using the knowledge they had that there were 10 beans in each cup.
Level 3. The children counted 40 beans by tens and then counted the rest by ones. Some of them used implicit or explicit multiplication and said, "Four tens is forty," or "Four times 10 is forty."

It can be seen in Table 2.2 that only 9 second graders (60%) counted the 48 beans correctly by tens. It also can be seen that the proportion counting by tens increased with age. Children count objects by using the num-

Table 2.2: Performance on Beans Task (by number of children)

	Level of Performance		
Grade	1	2	3
2	2	4	9
3	0	4	11
4	1	1	13
5	0	0	15
Total	3	9	48

$n = 15$ for each grade

chi-square = 11.0; $df = 6$; $p < .0884$

From *The Development of Children's Place-Value Numeration Concepts in Grades Two through Five*, by S. H. Ross, 1986, paper presented at the annual meeting of the American Educational Research Association, San Francisco, p. 17. Reprinted with permission.

bers they have constructed in their heads, and if they have only *ones* in their heads, as shown in Figure 2.2(a), they can count only by *ones*. They can count by *tens* in this situation only if they have *tens* in their heads, as shown in Figure 2.2(b).

It is possible to teach children to count by tens. However, many children find 300 lima beans by counting as shown in Figure 2.3. These children have been taught to count by tens but cannot shift to ones after "forty" because, to shift to ones, they have to have been thinking *simultaneously* about *tens* and *ones*. This ability to think at two hierarchical levels simultaneously is logico-mathematical knowledge. How second graders in our classrooms construct this logico-mathematical knowledge is the topic to which we now turn.

The system of tens has to be constructed by each child out of his or her own system of ones. The best way to encourage children to begin to do this is to encourage them to *think*. For example, when they have to think of a "quick and easy way" to deal with 9 + 6, they will think about a *ten* and *ones* simultaneously if they know that 9 + 1 = 10. As can be seen in Chapter 6, one of the ways they invent is (9 + 1) + 5. If they are later asked for a way to deal with 19 + 6, they are likely to invent (19 + 1) + 5 or [10 + (9 + 1) + 5]. When they get to 29 + 36, they may do 20 + 30 = 50, 9 + 6 = 15, and 50 + 15 = 65; or they may change the problem to 30 + 35. When children thus struggle to *think* about *tens* and *ones simultaneously*, they are encouraged to build the mental structure illustrated in Figure 2.2(b).

Second graders already have the social knowledge that the way to write "ten" is "10," and that the way to write "twenty" is "20," and so on.

Figure 2.3. How some children count 48 beans by not shifting to *ones* after "forty."

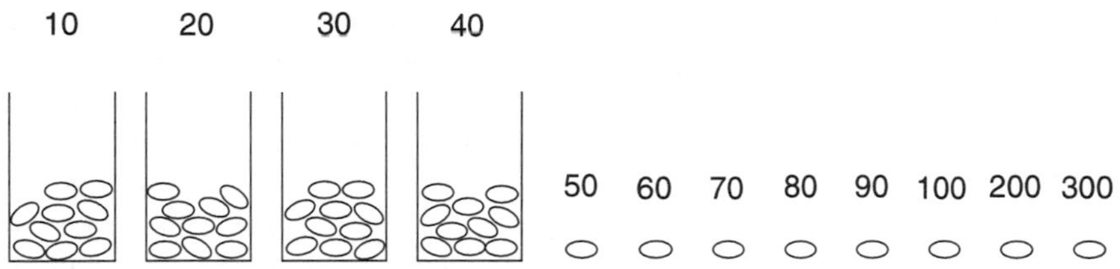

In Chapter 6, we will show how the teacher writes and erases parts of two-digit numbers as children construct the logico-mathematical knowledge of tens and ones.

Figure 2.2(b) shows why base-ten blocks and 10 straws bundled together with a rubber band cannot empirically teach children to think "one ten" and "ten ones" *simultaneously*. By looking at a long stick with 10 segments or 10 straws bundled together, the child can think "one ten" and "ten ones" only at two different times. Adults already have the logico-mathematical knowledge of tens and ones, and this is why we can see "one ten" and "ten ones" simultaneously in a ten block.

HOW IS PLACE VALUE UNLEARNED?

When we wrote the first edition of this book in the late 1980s, we had no idea that the teaching of "carrying" and "borrowing" had the effect of "unteaching" place value. We knew that students transferring from other schools clung to the algorithms they could not explain and that their knowledge of place value was very poor. In dealing with

$$\begin{array}{r} 15 \\ + 27 \\ \hline \end{array},$$

for example, the children who had been at our school since kindergarten did 10 + 20 = 30 first because they had never been taught to do 5 + 7 first. The students who transferred to our school in second grade had already been taught to add the ones first and continued to use this method. We noticed, however, that the cognitively very advanced transfer students quickly began to add the tens first. Those in the "normal" range or below, however, continued to "carry" for a long time—until January, March, or beyond.

By May 1990, we had hypothesized that algorithms were the cause of children's poor knowledge of place value, and we interviewed all the second graders at our school, using a variety of computational problems. In May 1991, using similar problems, we interviewed the same children at the end of third grade, as well as four classes of fourth graders. An analysis of these and many other interviews clearly indicated that algorithms are harmful to children, and Chapter 3 of *Young Children Continue to Reinvent Arithmetic, 3rd Grade* (Kamii, 1994) was entitled "The Harmful Effects of Algorithms."

In retrospect, we should have thought about the harmful effects of algorithms when we wrote the first edition of this volume. However, we were blind to this possibility and believed that children who invented their own procedures were just better than the traditionally instructed children. In other words, we assumed that algorithms were good for children but that our method was better for them. We also assumed that place value was very hard for young children and never thought that instruction in a public school could be harmful to them. Many data can be presented to prove the harmful effects of algorithms, but we will limit ourselves to children's reactions to five problems.

7 + 52 + 186

There were three classes of second graders at our school in May 1990, and all the children in the three classes were individually interviewed. One of the problems given in the mental-arithmetic interview was 7 + 52 + 186 presented twice—once in vertical form and later in horizontal form. The three classes did not differ very much when the question was written vertically, but striking differences emerged when the same problem was presented horizontally.

All the answers to the horizontally written problem given by the three classes are listed in Table 2.3. The teacher of the first class (labeled "Algorithms") taught algorithms, but the teachers of the other two classes did not. The two classes differed, however, in that only the teacher (LJ) who had the class labeled "No algorithms" immediately called parents at home when children were taught to "carry" and to "borrow."

Most of the students in the "No algorithms" class typically began by saying, "One hundred eighty and fifty is two hundred and thirty" and then added the ones. This is why nearly four times as many children in the "No algorithms" class got the correct answer as those in the class labeled "Algorithms" (45% compared with 12%).

Much more informative were the *incorrect* answers the children gave. The two dotted lines across Table 2.3 were drawn to indicate a range of incorrect but reasonable answers. All the incorrect answers given by the "Algorithms" class were above and below this range and revealed poor number sense and knowledge of place value. For example, three children

Table 2.3: Answers to 7 + 52 + 186 Given by Three Classes of Second Graders in May 1990

Algorithms $n = 17$	Some algorithms taught at home $n = 19$	No algorithms $n = 20$
9308		
1000		
989		
986		
938	989	
906	938	
838	810	
295	356	617
		255
		246
245 (12%)	245 (26%)	245 (45%)
		243
		236
		235
200	213	138
198	213	—
30	199	—
29	133	—
29	125	—
—	114	
—	—	
	—	
	—	

Note: Dashes indicate that the child declined to try to work the problem.

in the "Algorithms" class got 29 or 30 for 7 + 52 + 186. These children added all the digits as *ones* (7 + 5 + 2 + 1 + 8 + 6 = 29). Many in the same class gave answers like 9308, 938, and 838 by proceeding from right to left and doing something like 2 + 6 = 8, 5 + 8 = 13, carry 1, and 1 + 7 + 1 = 9. A characteristic of this class was the children's emotional flatness, and the fact that no one seemed to feel anything wrong with answers in the 800s, 900s, and beyond. The children seemed to be functioning like machines, without any intuition or number sense.

The children in the "No algorithms" class also made errors, but their wrong answers were more reasonable because most of them got to 230 by beginning with 180 + 50 = 230, as stated earlier. The errors they made were mostly in dealing with the ones. The child who produced the answer of 617 was taught algorithms at home by parents who had said that they would stop this instruction.

The class labeled "Some algorithms taught at home" in Table 2.3 came out between the other two classes. The percentage getting the correct answer was 26, which was between 12% and 45%. The range of incorrect answers was not as outlandish as in the "Algorithms" class but not as reasonable as in the "No algorithms" class.

All the second graders were mixed before going to third grade and divided into three heterogeneous classes as randomly as possible. In May 1991, a similar problem, 6 + 53 + 185, was given to all the third- and fourth-grade classes; the results are presented in Tables 2.4 and 2.5.

Only one of the three third-grade teachers was a "No algorithms" teacher. Although she had 20 students in her class, only 13 of them had never been taught any algorithms at school, and 3 of the 13 were absent

Table 2.4: Answers to 6 + 53 + 185 Given by Three Classes of Third Graders in May 1991

Algorithms $n = 19$	Algorithms $n = 20$	No algorithms $n = 10$
	800 + 38	
838	800	
768	444	
533	344	284
246		245
244 (32%)	244 (20%)	244 (50%)
235	243	243
234	239	238
	238	
	234	
213	204	221
194	202	
194	190	
74	187	
29	144	
—	139	
—	—	
	—	

Note: Dashes indicate that the child declined to try to work the problem.

Table 2.5: Answers to 6 + 53 + 185 Given by Four Classes of Fourth Graders in May 1991

Algorithms $n = 20$	Algorithms $n = 21$	Algorithms $n = 21$	Algorithms $n = 18$
	1215		
	848		
	844		
	783		
1300	783		10,099
814	783		838
744	718	791	835
715	713	738	745
713 + 8	445	721	274
	245		
244 (30%)	244 (24%)	244 (19%)	244 (17%)
243	234		234
	224		234
			234
194	194	144	225
177	127	138	"8, 3, 8"
144	—	134	"4, 3, 2"
143	—	"8, 3, 7"	"4, 3, 2"
134		"8, 1, 7"	—
"4, 4, 4"		—	—
"1, 3, 2"		—	—
		—	
		—	
		—	
		—	
		—	
		—	

Note: Dashes indicate that the child declined to try to work the problem.

on the day of the interview. It can be observed again that the "No algorithms" group produced the correct answer more often (50%) than the two "Algorithms" classes (32% and 20%, respectively). The incorrect answers of the "No algorithms" class were also much more reasonable than the wrong answers produced by the "Algorithms" classes.

All the fourth-grade teachers taught algorithms in 1990–91, and the children in Table 2.5 had been taught algorithms for 1 to 4 years. As far as the proportion getting the correct answer is concerned, we can see that all the fourth-grade classes did worse than the second and third graders who had never been taught any algorithms (30%, 24%, 19%, and 17%, compared with 45% and 50%). The incorrect answers produced by the fourth graders were as outlandish as those of the "Algorithms" third graders, but a new symptom appeared: answers such as "Eight, three, seven," indicating that each column remained separate in these children's minds, from right to left. These students not only had inadequate knowledge of place value but also thought about each column as an isolated column, and did not even bother to read the answer as "seven hundred thirty-eight."

By fourth grade, we expected children at least to be bothered if they got answers greater than 400 or smaller than 200. However, none of those who produced incorrect answers showed any sign of hesitation, and 19% said they could not add the three numbers without a pencil. The fourth graders who had been taught algorithms for 1 to 4 years thus can be said to have done considerably worse than the second graders who were not taught these rules.

22 + 7 in First Grade

Several years later in early May, one of us (CK) interviewed 37 children in 2 first-grade classes, and one of the problems given was the following:

$$\begin{array}{r} 22 \\ + 7 \\ \hline \end{array}$$

The two classes had been receiving traditional math instruction, and one of the teachers had taught the algorithm for two-digit addition without regrouping. As can be seen in Table 2.6, 67% of the class that had not been taught the algorithm produced the correct answer, but only 37% of the "Algorithm" class did.

Most of the errors made by the "No algorithm" class were 24, 25, 27, or 28. These errors were much more reasonable than answers like 11, which

$$\begin{array}{c} 22 \\ \end{array}$$

Table 2.6: Answers to $\underline{+\ 7}$ Given by Two Classes of First Graders in the Same School

Answers given	Algorithm taught $n = 19$	Algorithm not taught $n = 18$
29	7 (37%)	12 (67%)
24, 25, 27, or 28	1 (5%)	4 (22%)
11	6 (32%)	0 (0%)
10 or 12	2 (11%)	0 (0%)
"9 and 2, 92"	1 (5%)	0 (0%)
"a 2 and a 9"	1 (5%)	0 (0%)
9	1 (5%)	0 (0%)
Stuck after 2 + 2 = 4	0 (0%)	1 (6%)
Sits silently and ends up agreeing to skip problem		1 (6%)

was given by 32% of the "Algorithm" class. Since the children in the "No algorithm" class counted-on from 22, their errors were larger than 22. By contrast, 53% (32% + 11% + 5% + 5%) of the "Algorithm" class got answers smaller than 22, essentially because they treated all the digits as ones. About a third of the "Algorithm" class got the answer of 11 by doing 2 + 2 + 7 = 11. We were surprised to learn that a few short lessons on double-column addition can cause first graders to unlearn the little they knew about place value.

13
x 4 in Third Grade

In the spring of 1992, we individually interviewed 13 third graders at our school, who had never been taught algorithms at school, and 39 third graders in another school where math was traditionally taught. The interviewer wrote the multiplication problem on a blank sheet of paper and asked each child to "work this problem," offering a pen. When the child finished writing the answer, the interviewer brought out a bagful of chips and asked, "If we make four piles of 13, 13, 13, and 13 chips (indicating four different locations on the table in front of the child), will we have what this problem says?" All the children replied in the affirmative, and four piles of 13 chips were made together. The interviewer then asked, "If we pushed all these together, how many chips would we have?" All the children replied, "Fifty-two," and the interviewer asked each child to explain with the chips (which were still in four piles of 13 each) "how all this works," pointing to what the child had written.

If the child showed only 4 chips (oooo) to explain 4 × 1, the interviewer remarked, "You used all these [pointing to the chips the child had used to explain 4 × 3 and 4 × 1] to explain how 'all this' works [pointing to the child's writing]. But you didn't use any of these [pointing to the unused chips]. Were you supposed to use all of them, or were you not supposed to?" The interviewer thus asked questions that might prompt a better explanation if the child did not adequately explain the written procedure on his or her own.

As can be seen in Table 2.7, all the children in both groups wrote the correct answer of 52. Almost all the children (97%) in the comparison group used the algorithm, while none in the constructivist group did. The proportion who adequately explained all the steps of their written computation was 92% for the constructivist group and only 5% for the comparison group (a difference significant at the .001 level). The inability of the comparison group to explain the algorithm they had used correctly was due mostly to their poor knowledge of place value. Eighty-seven percent interpreted the 1 of 13 as a *one* and showed only four chips (oooo) to explain the 4 × 1 part. It was truly amazing that when asked whether all 52 of the chips had to be used to explain the algorithm, these third graders said that it was not necessary to use all of them.

32
− 18 in Third Grade

This subtraction problem was given immediately after the preceding multiplication problem. After the child finished writing the answer, the interviewer put all the chips in front of the child saying, "I'd like you to explain with these chips how all this works that you wrote. Let's count out 32 chips

Table 2.7: Percentages in the Constructivist and Comparison Groups
Explaining How They Got the Answer to $\frac{13}{\times\ 4}$

	Constructivist group ($n = 13$)	Comparison group ($n = 39$)	Difference	Significance (1-tailed)
Correct answer (52)	100	100	0	
Use of algorithm	0	97	97	.001
Adequate explanation of all the steps	92	5	87	.001
Interpreting the "1" of "13" as a one	0	87	87	.001

for this number that you had before taking 18 away [pointing to the 32 on the paper]."

Eighty-five percent of the constructivist group and 97% of the comparison group got the correct answer of 14 (see Table 2.8). Of those who produced the correct answer, 100% of the constructivist group and only 21% of the comparison group could explain how they got this answer. The difficulty of the comparison group was again due mostly to poor knowledge of place value. They used three chips (ooo) to explain how "borrowing one from three" and "taking one away from two" worked.

17
+ 16 in Second Grade

In the spring of 2002, I (CK) gave this problem to two groups of low-SES second graders in California. The students in the constructivist group had been in the lowest math group at the beginning of first grade. They were then at such a low cognitive level that they could not conserve number or tell how many of four counters the interviewer had hidden. These children received constructivist instruction in first and second grades and were, of course, not taught any algorithms. This group of second graders was compared with a similar group in another school in the same low-SES neighborhood. In that school, math was taught with a state-approved textbook and workbook that included algorithms. To have a comparison group of about the same size, I asked for six low-performing students from 4 second-grade classes. (This request was made because

Table 2.8: Percentages in the Constructivist and Comparison Groups
Explaining How They Got the Answer to $\dfrac{32}{-18}$

	Constructivist group ($n = 13$)	Comparison group ($n = 39$)	Difference	Significance (1-tailed)
Correct answer (14)	85	97	12	n.s.
Use of algorithm	0	100	100	.001
Adequate explanation of all the steps (percentages only of those who got the correct answer)	100	21	79	.001
Interpreting the tens as ones	0	87	87	.001

low-performing first graders usually become low-performing second graders.)

As can be seen in Table 2.9, significantly more students in the constructivist group wrote the correct answer of 33 (86% vs. 52%). When asked to explain their written procedures with a pile of 17 counters and another of 16, none of the group who had been taught algorithms could explain "carrying." By contrast, most (57%) of the constructivist group explained their procedures with tens and ones. (The others counted-on by ones.)

Second and Third Graders' Knowledge of the "1" in "17"

I showed a card on which "17" had been written to the same groups of second graders just discussed and asked each child to count out "this many" counters. I then circled the "7" and asked each child to show me with the chips "what this part means" and then circled the "1," asking "what this part means."

As can be seen in Table 2.10, 67% of the second graders in the constructivist group and only 4% of those in the comparison group showed 10 chips to explain the meaning of the "1" in "17." The difference between the two groups was significant at the .001 level.

Table 2.10 also shows third graders' knowledge of the "1" in "17." The third graders in the constructivist group had been in the lowest math group in first grade and had had 3 years of constructivist math without any algorithms. The third graders in the comparison group consisted of about four low-performing students from each of four classes, and these students had had 3 years of algorithms.

It can be seen in Table 2.10 that 100% of the constructivist group showed 10 counters to indicate the meaning of the "1" in "17." By contrast, only 35% of the comparison group indicated this knowledge ($p < .001$). The

Table 2.9: Numbers and Percentages of Two Groups of Second Graders Solving 17 + 16

	Constructivist group ($n = 21$)	Comparison group ($n = 23$)	Difference	Significance (1-tailed)
Correct answer (33)	18 (86%)	12 (52%)	34%	.01
Use of algorithm	2 (10%)	13 (57%)	47%	.001
Perfect explanation with tens and ones	12 (57%)	0 (0%)	57%	.001

Table 2.10: Numbers and Percentages of Two Groups of Second and Third
Graders Showing 10 Chips for the "1" in "17"

	Constructivist group [a]	Comparison group [b]	Difference	Significance (1-tailed)
Second grade	14 (67%)	1 (4%)	63%	.001
Third grade	12 (100%)	6 (35%)	65%	.001

[a] $n = 21$ for second grade; $n = 12$ for third grade

[b] $n = 23$ for second grade; $n = 17$ for third grade

fact that 100% of the third graders in the constructivist group demonstrated knowledge of place value proves that even low-performing, low-SES children can learn place value if they are not taught any algorithms.

CONCLUSION

Many more data on the harmful effects of teaching algorithms can be found in Chapter 10 of the present volume and Chapters 3 and 13 of *Young Children Continue to Reinvent Arithmetic, 3rd Grade* (Kamii, 1994). In conclusion, algorithms are harmful for two reasons: (1) They make children give up their own thinking, and (2) they "unteach" place value, thereby preventing children from developing number sense.

As stated earlier, children proceed from left to right when they do their own thinking in multidigit addition and subtraction. Because there is no compromise possible between going toward the right and going toward the left as the algorithms require, children have to give up their own thinking to obey the teacher. We have noted children's emotional flatness and lack of intuition when they get 29 or 900 for 7 + 52 + 186. These are symptoms of children who have given up their own thinking and are functioning like machines.

The algorithm of "carrying" serves to "unteach" place value by encouraging children to think about every digit as ones. In dealing with a problem like

$$\begin{array}{r} 48 \\ + 25 \\ \hline \end{array},$$

for example, children say, "Eight and five is thirteen. Put down the three; carry the one. One and four is five, plus two is seven." The algorithm is convenient for adults, who already know that the "4" and the "2" stand for 40 and 20. For second graders, who have a tendency to think about all the digits as ones, however, the algorithm serves to reinforce this error, as we saw in the examples given earlier.

There are a few second graders who are cognitively more advanced than the majority, know tens very well, and are therefore not harmed by the rules of "carrying." Adults certainly do not unlearn place value when they say, "One and four is five, plus two is seven," in the preceding situation. However, the great majority of second graders think "one," "four," and "two" when they say these words.

The harmful effects of algorithms have been suspected since the 1970s and 1980s (Carraher, Carraher, & Schliemann, 1985; Carraher & Schliemann, 1985; Jones, 1975; Plunkett, 1979). By the 1990s, an increasing number of educators were saying that the teaching of algorithms was harmful to children (Kamii, 1994; McNeal, 1995; Narode, Board, & Davenport, 1993; Pack, 1997; Parker, 1993; Richardson, 1996). However, authors of textbooks are still advocating the teaching of these rules, and "education reform" seems to mean only more testing, without any improvement in how we teach children. We conclude by wondering whether it will take 10 or 20 more years for algorithms to disappear from second-grade math books.

CHAPTER 3

The Importance of Social Interaction

EDUCATORS OFTEN SAY that peer interaction is important because children learn from each other. We agree that children learn many things from each other, but this is not our reason for advocating social interaction among peers in math classes. Logico-mathematical knowledge has its source inside each child and is elaborated through each child's own mental actions. In the logico-mathematical realm, therefore, other people are not the sources of knowledge. Rather, other people's ideas are important because they provide occasions for children to think critically about their own ideas in relation to other people's. For example, if one child says that $5 + 4 = 8$, and another says that $5 + 4 = 9$, this disagreement leads to critical thinking by both children, through the exchange of viewpoints. When children are convinced that someone else's idea makes better sense than theirs, they change their minds and correct themselves, *from the inside*.

Piaget (1980b) attributed great importance to social interaction. To him, such exchanges were indispensable, both for children's elaboration of logical thought and for adults' construction of sciences. As he put it:

> Certain educators say sometimes that my theory is only "cognitive" and that I neglected the importance of social aspects of the child's development. It is true that most of my publications have dealt with various aspects of cognitive development, particularly the development of operativity, but in my first works I emphasized the importance of interindividual exchanges sufficiently not to feel the need afterwards to return to it. In fact, it is clear that the confrontation of points of view is already indispensable in childhood for the elaboration of logical thought, and such confrontations become increasingly more important in the elaboration of sciences by adults. Without the diversity of theories and the constant search for going beyond the contradictions among them, scientific progress would not have been possible. (p. vii)

Piaget did not experimentally verify his theory about the importance of social interaction, but other researchers at the University of Geneva did. We have selected two studies by Doise and Mugny (1981/1984) as examples for this chapter. They demonstrate that even a 10-minute debate by two people whose ideas are equally wrong can result in the construction of higher-level logic.

EXCHANGE BETWEEN CHILD AND ADULT

Experimental Conditions

For their studies of the effects of social interaction on children's development of logic, Doise and Mugny (1981/1984) selected a task involving the conservation of length. Two rails 4 cm wide and 22 cm long were used in the experimental sessions. Some toy wagons were also available at the beginning of the experiment, so that the child could play with the material and understand the meaning of the rails.

The two rails were first placed in visual correspondence as shown in Figure 3.1(a), and the child judged them to be the same in length. One of the rails was then pushed slightly to the right (see Figure 3.l(b)), and the child was asked if the rails had the same length or if one was longer than the other. Since all the children included in this study were nonconservers, with a mean age of 6 years, 3 months, they all said at this point that one rail was longer than the other. When asked to explain their answer, they said that one of the rails stuck out beyond the other one. This is a typical response. Nonconservers usually focus on the point of arrival of the stick that was pushed and compare that end with the end of the other stick, without paying attention to the point of departure.

Figure 3.1. Successive configurations in the conservation-of-equal-length task.

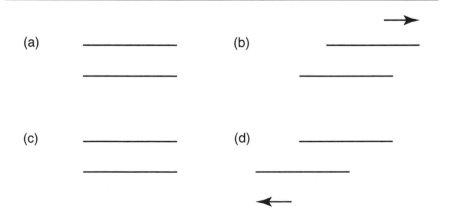

Doise and Mugny ideally wanted to conduct this experiment with pairs of children who would disagree in two different ways. More specifically, they wanted to compare the outcomes of the following three conditions, two of which involved a stooge:

1. *The stooge would give an equally incorrect answer.* The nonconserver would exchange points of view with a stooge who would disagree by giving an equally wrong answer at the same cognitive level. If the non-conserving child said the top rail in Figure 3.1(b) was longer, this condition required the stooge to say, "I think the bottom rail is longer because it sticks out right here [at the opposite end]." The stooge's answer would always be the opposite of the subject's, and the two answers would be equally wrong, at the same cognitive level. The experimenter would then say to the two people that there seemed to be a disagreement and ask them to "talk it over" to see if they could come to an agreement.
2. *The stooge would give the correct answer.* The nonconserver would exchange points of view with a stooge who would disagree by giving the correct answer. In this condition, the stooge would say, "I think the two rails have the same length because the top rail sticks out on this side but the bottom rail sticks out on the other side. That's why I think the two rails have the same length." The experimenter would then encourage the child and stooge to talk to each other and consider one another's point of view. (Unlike in the previous condition, the stooge's idea would be at a higher cognitive level than the child's.)
3. *No stooge would be involved (the control group).* The nonconserver would not exchange points of view in this condition and would work alone with the experimenter. The questions put to him or her would be the same as in the other two conditions, but the number of items would be doubled to fill up the same amount of time as in the other two conditions.

Since it was impossible to expect a 6-year-old to act as a stooge, Doise and Mugny decided to use an adult for this experiment. In the first two conditions, therefore, there were two adults and a child. The stooge responded differently to the different statements the subject made. For example, if the subject in the first experimental condition adopted the stooge's incorrect answer, which was often the case, the stooge shifted to the child's initial response by saying, "But I agree with you that this one is longer," pointing to the rail initially chosen by the child. If, on the other hand, the child in this same situation switched to the correct answer, the stooge repeated the wrong answer. When the child persisted in giving the correct answer, the experimenter decided to go on to the next item or to stop the experiment without spending 5 minutes per item, as originally planned.

Pretest, First Posttest, and Second Posttest

As stated earlier, the children who participated in this study were all nonconservers on the pretest. Those who were either conservers or inter- mediates were excluded from the study. The first posttest was given im- mediately after the experimental session was finished. A second posttest was given 10 days later to evaluate the stability of the gains.

The pretest, first posttest, and second posttest all consisted of two con- servation tasks that were individually administered. One involved rods of equal length, and the other one involved chains of unequal length. These tasks were given as follows.

Conservation of Equal Lengths. The child was shown two wooden rods of the same color, each 10 cm long. "These are sticks, but let's pretend they are roads," the experimenter said. As she placed the sticks in visual corre- spondence, shown in Figure 3.1(a), she ran her finger along one rod and asked, "Do you think here you'd have to walk as much as on the other road?" running her finger along the other stick. If the child did not under- stand the question, the experimenter repeated it with reference to an ant: "Do you think an ant would have to walk as much here as here? Or do you think it would have a longer way to go on one of the roads?" The child was then asked about length: "Do you think the sticks both have the same length? Or do you think there is one that is longer than the other?" (All these questions were carefully asked because young children often say that the roads are the same but not the lengths. For many young chil- dren, length refers to the point of arrival of the rod, and not to the dis- tance from the point of departure to the point of arrival.)

The same kinds of questions were posed with all four of the configura- tions shown in Figure 3.1. In (a) the two rods are in visual correspondence. In (b) one rod has been pushed to the right. The rod is returned to its origi- nal position in (c), and the other rod has been pushed to the left in (d).

The children were categorized into three groups after the pretest, first posttest, and second posttest: conservers, nonconservers, and intermedi- ates. Conservers judged the two rods as having the same length in all four of the situations shown in Figure 3.1. When asked to justify their answers, they confidently gave arguments such as, "All you did was move this one, and we can put it back to the way it was before" or "This rod sticks out on this end, but the other rod sticks out on the other end; so the length is the same."

Nonconservers said that the roads had the same length in (a) and (c) of Figure 3.1, but, when a rod was moved as shown in (b) and (d), they said that one was longer than the other. Usually but not always, they said that the one that had been pushed in either direction was longer and explained that it stuck out beyond the one that had not been pushed.

Among the children classified as intermediates were those who gave correct answers but could not justify them. Others in this category gave the correct answer on one item but not on the other. Still others vacillated and kept changing their minds.

Conservation of Unequal Lengths. Two chains were used in this task, a 10-cm chain and a 15-cm chain. They were presented in the configurations shown in Figure 3.2, and the children were asked questions similar to those described earlier.

Conservers confidently judged the 15-cm chain to be longer in all four of the situations in Figure 3.2. They also could justify their judgments logically.

Nonconservers said in situation (b) that the two chains had the same length, and that the ant would walk as much on one road as on the other. Their justification for making this statement was that the extremities of the roads coincided. In situation (d), the nonconservers said that the bottom road was longer because it stuck out beyond the other. Nonconservers maintained this response, even when they were reminded of their previous statement that the top road was longer.

Figure 3.2. Successive configurations in the conservation-of-unequal-length task.

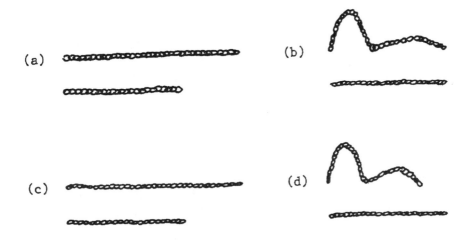

(a)

(b)

(c)

(d)

The intermediates usually said that the 15-cm chain was longer in situation (b) but not in situation (d). They also had trouble justifying their correct answer. In addition, their responses were characterized by hesitation and vacillation.

Results

As stated before, all the participants in this study were nonconservers on the pretest. By comparing the frequencies of the first posttest and the second posttest, Doise and Mugny determined whether children made more advances under condition 1, 2, or 3. The data are presented in Table 3.1.

The first point that can be made is that the nonconservers who exchanged points of view with a stooge made considerably more progress than those in the control group, who were exposed only to the material and questions. On the first posttest, all 13 of the children in the control group remained nonconservers on the conservation-of-equal-length task, and 12 of the 13 remained nonconservers on the conservation-of-unequal-length task. On the second posttest, these figures had changed very little, to 12 and 10, respectively. By contrast, at least half of those in the two other groups made progress by becoming intermediates or conservers.

Table 3.1: Results of Nonconservers' Exchanges of Viewpoints with an Adult

	Equal Length			Unequal Length		
	Non-conserver	Inter-mediate	Conserver	Non-conserver	Inter-mediate	Conserver
First posttest						
Incorrect answer ($n = 20$)	11	1	8	7	5	8
Correct answer ($n = 19$)	1	2	16	10	5	4
Control ($n = 13$)	13	0	0	12	1	0
Second posttest						
Incorrect answer ($n = 20$)	11	2	7	5	8	7
Correct answer ($n = 19$)	2	4	13	8	6	5
Control ($n = 13$)	12	1	0	10	2	1

Adapted from *The Social Development of the Intellect* (pp. 86–87), by W. Doise and G. Mugny, 1981/1984, New York: Pergamon.

It may not be surprising to find out that the children who were exposed to the correct answer made progress. The surprising and significant finding of this study is that disagreeing with an adult who gave an equally incorrect answer at the same cognitive level was beneficial. If we take the conservation-of-unequal-length task as the more stringent test, we can see in Table 3.1 that, on the first posttest, the children who were confronted with an incorrect answer made slightly more gains than those who were confronted with the correct answer (8/20 compared with 4/19 became conservers, and 5/20 compared with 5/19 became intermediates). By the second posttest, even more children had made gains, with the incorrect-answer group still in the lead (7/20 compared with 5/19 became conservers, and 8/20 compared with 6/19 became intermediates).

A transmission-and-internalization theory of math education could not explain why children can make advances in logic when they exchange viewpoints with an adult who has an equally wrong but different answer. However, Piaget's constructivism states that children construct higher-level logic from the inside, out of the lower levels they have already constructed. In the situation in Figure 3.1(b), for example, it is equally incorrect to think that the top rod is longer as it is to think that the bottom rod is longer. The only way to resolve this conflict is to construct a higher level that *includes both of the lower-level ideas.* When the nonconservers tried to reconcile the contradiction between their idea and the stooge's, they coordinated the opposing viewpoints and constructed a higher-level relationship that included the opposing viewpoints.

The gains of the group exposed to the correct answer are considerable. The gains made by this group on the equal-length task can be explained by constructivism or by a transmission-and-internalization theory. However, the progress made on the unequal-length task can be explained only by Piaget's constructivism. Exposing children to the correct answer produced more correct answers on the equal-length task (16/19 compared with 8/20 on the first posttest, and 13/19 compared with 7/20 on the second posttest). However, the data about the unequal-length task give us reason to be skeptical about such quick gains.

EXCHANGE BETWEEN PAIRS OF CHILDREN

The preceding experiment was one of four in a series reported by Doise and Mugny (1981/1984). Another experiment will now be described because it involves the exchange of viewpoints between pairs of children, rather than between an adult and a child.

Experimental Conditions

There were two conditions in this experiment, the results of which are shown in Table 3.2. In the first, the control condition, the children were questioned individually in a way similar to the third condition in the previous study. In the second condition, the children were interviewed in pairs. The two children sat face to face across a table and were asked to exchange points of view and to come to an agreement if they disagreed. If, throughout the experiment, there was no evidence of disagreement on an audiotape, the children were assigned to the category called "without conflict." If there was recorded evidence of disagreement at some point during the experiment, the children were assigned to the category called "with conflict."

Results

As in the previous study, all the children who participated were those who were found to be nonconservers on the pretest. The tasks used in the pretest, first posttest, and second posttest were the same as in the experiment with an adult stooge.

As can be seen in Table 3.2, only one pair in the control group made progress. The pairs that made the most progress were those who disagreed and exchanged ideas in an attempt to come to an agreement. Eleven out of the 18 pairs of children "with conflict" made progress, both on the equal-length and unequal-length tasks. By contrast, only 4 and 6 pairs of children, respectively, out of 18 pairs "without conflict" made progress on the

Table 3.2: Results of Exchanges of Viewpoints Among Pairs of Nonconserving Children

	Equal Length			Unequal Length		
	Non-conserver	Inter-mediate	Conserver	Non-conserver	Inter-mediate	Conserver
Posttest						
Individual controls ($n = 12$)	11	0	1	11	1	0
Pairs without conflict ($n = 18$)	14	3	1	12	6	0
Pairs with conflict ($n = 18$)	7	10	1	7	10	1

Adapted from *The Social Development of the Intellect* (p. 94), by W. Doise and G. Mugny, 1981/1984, New York: Pergamon.

equal-length and unequal-length tasks. These gains were very stable on the second posttest, according to Doise and Mugny (1981/1984).

The authors speculated about the modest gains made by the pairs of children who did not disagree, as far as they could determine from the audiotape. They hypothesized that the children who did not verbally challenge each other nevertheless may have exchanged viewpoints in nonverbal ways.

CONCLUSION

The experimental studies cited in this chapter are too small and too few in number to be convincing by themselves. The importance of social interaction, however, can be gleaned from many other experiments reported by Doise and Mugny (1981/1984), as well as Perret-Clermont (1979/1980, described in part by Kamii, 2000). Evidence of the importance of the exchange of viewpoints also can be found in the long history of mathematics and the physical sciences (Kuhn, 1970; Piaget, 1980b; Piaget & Garcia, 1983/1989). As was pointed out in Chapter 1, science is a social enterprise, and the acceptance of a scientific truth is a social phenomenon. If adults construct mathematics and science by debating points of conflict, children, too, can be expected to construct logico-mathematical knowledge by the same process. The experiments discussed in this chapter took only about 10 minutes, but the findings can be extrapolated to the outcome of 10 years of schooling. The *Principles and Standards for School Mathematics* (National Council of Teachers of Mathematics, 2000) went quite far in advocating communication, and we hope the next revision will advocate debates rather than mere communication.

The importance of social interaction is discussed further in the next chapter, dealing with autonomy as the aim of education. The history of mathematics and the science attests to the intellectual autonomy of the human species. Human beings construct knowledge by trying to make ever better sense of their experiences. We are not passive vessels who can hold only the knowledge that is poured into our heads.

PART II

Goals and Objectives

CHAPTER 4

Autonomy: The Aim of Education for Piaget

MANY SCHOOLS NOWADAYS have metal detectors and separate time slots set aside for conflict resolution, drug prevention, and AIDS prevention. Some schools even have 10–30 minutes a week of "character education," as if morality could be transmitted to children in small, weekly doses. All these sociomoral issues are part of autonomy and heteronomy, which are fostered every minute of the school day, whether or not we are aware of this.

In the intellectual realm, we have separate programs of testing with coercive consequences and/or monetary rewards for teachers. Test mania, too, reinforces children and teachers' heteronomy in the name of "accountability" and "education reform." Perhaps 20 years from now, we will look back on these band-aid approaches and marvel at the backwardness of all these efforts.

We begin this chapter by reviewing what Piaget (1932/1965) meant by autonomy and heteronomy and discuss what he said (Piaget, 1948/1973) about autonomy as the aim of education.

WHAT IS AUTONOMY,
AND HOW DOES IT DEVELOP?

Autonomy means being governed by oneself. It is the opposite of heteronomy, which means being governed by somebody else. Autonomy in Piaget's theory does not refer to the political *right* to make decisions, as it does when we say "Palestinian autonomy." In Piaget's theory, autonomy means the *ability* to make decisions for oneself, about right and wrong in the moral realm and about truth and untruth in the intellectual realm, by taking relevant factors into account, independently of reward and punishment. We first will discuss moral autonomy and then go on to clarify what Piaget meant by intellectual autonomy.

Moral Autonomy

An unusual example of moral autonomy is Martin Luther King's struggle
for civil rights. By taking relevant factors into account, such as the welfare of all citizens, King became convinced that the laws discriminating
against African Americans were immoral. Thus, he systematically challenged the discriminatory laws in spite of the arrests, police brutality, dogs,
water hoses, and threats of assassination used to stop him. A morally autonomous person is governed by what he or she believes to be right, and
not by reward and punishment.

An example of moral heteronomy is the Watergate coverup affair. The
men under President Nixon were governed by him and went along with
what they knew to be morally wrong, reaping the rewards the president
dispensed to those who helped him in the coverup attempt.

In *The Moral Judgment of the Child*, Piaget (1932/1965) gave more com-
monplace examples of autonomy and heteronomy. He interviewed children between the ages of 6 and 14 and asked them, for example, why it
was bad to tell lies. Young, heteronomous children replied, "Because you
get punished when you tell lies." "Would it be OK to tell lies if you were
not punished for them?" Piaget asked, and young children answered "Yes."
He went on to ask, "Which is worse, telling a lie to an adult or to another
child?" Young, heteronomous children responded that it was worse to lie
to an adult. Why? "Because adults can tell when something is not true."
Older, more autonomous children tended to say that it was sometimes
necessary to lie to adults, but that it was rotten to do it to another child.

The important question for parents and teachers to ask is: What causes
certain children to become more autonomous than others? Piaget's answer to this question is that adults reinforce children's natural heteronomy
when they use reward and punishment, thereby hindering the development of autonomy. By refraining from using rewards and punishments,
and by exchanging points of view with children instead, we can foster the
development of autonomy, he said.

For example, if a child tells a lie, an adult can punish the child by depriving him or her of dessert. But, instead of punishing the child, the adult
can look the child straight in the eye with affection and skepticism and
say, "I *really* can't believe what you are saying because . . . [and give the
reason]. And when you tell me something next time, I am not sure I'll be
able to believe you, because I think you lied this time. I want you to go to
your room and think about what you might do next time."

Children who are raised with this kind of exchange of viewpoints are
likely, over time, to construct from within the value of honesty. Children
who are confronted with the fact that other people cannot believe them

are likely, over time, to construct from within the conclusion that it is best in the long run for people to be able to trust each other.

An essential element here is a warm human relationship of mutual respect and affection between the child and the adult. If children believe that an adult does not care about them anyway, they will have no reason to want to be believed.

In general, punishment leads to three possible outcomes. The first is calculation of risks. Children who are punished will learn to calculate their chances of getting caught the next time and the price they might have to pay if they are caught. While these calculations may be good for children in terms of learning about probability, their value for children's moral development is obviously questionable.

The second possible outcome of punishment is the opposite of the first one, namely, blind obedience. In our culture especially, sensitive little girls will do anything to avoid being punished, and this is how they give the impression that punishment works. When children become blindly obedient, they come to feel psychologically safe because they become respectable and do not have to make decisions any more. Rather than thinking about relevant factors, all these children have to do is to obey.

The third common outcome of punishment is a derivative of the second, namely, revolt. Many "good," model children surprise us eventually by beginning to cut classes, take drugs, and engage in other acts that characterize delinquency. Their reason for switching to these behaviors is that they are tired of living for their parents and teachers, and think the time has come for them to start living for themselves. While acts of revolt may look like autonomous acts, there is a vast difference between autonomy and revolt. In revolt, the child figures out what is expected and deliberately does the opposite. A child who always has to go counter to the norm is not autonomous.

Many behaviorists and others believe that punishment is bad because it is negative, but that rewards are positive and good. However, rewards do not make children any more autonomous than punishment. The child who fills out a worksheet only to get a sticker and the one who does chores only to get money are being manipulated by others just as much as the child who is "good" only to avoid being punished. The Watergate affair happened because the men under the president expected to be rewarded by him.

When adults exchange viewpoints with children, this exchange fosters the development of autonomy by enabling children to consider various perspectives. When children can take relevant factors into account, such as other people's rights and feelings, they construct from within the rule, for example, that it is better for human beings to deal honestly with each other. A person who has constructed this conviction cannot lie in situations like the Watergate affair, no matter what reward is offered. (For more about rewards, punishments, and sanctions by reciprocity, see Kamii, 2000, pp. 60–61.)

Intellectual Autonomy

In the intellectual realm, too, autonomy means governing oneself by being able to take relevant factors into account, and heteronomy means being governed by somebody else. An unusual example of intellectual autonomy is Copernicus, who promulgated the heliocentric theory in 1543, when everybody else believed that the sun revolved around the earth. The scientists of his time laughed at him and did not even let him finish his lectures. But Copernicus was autonomous enough to remain convinced of the truth of his theory.

An intellectually heteronomous person, by contrast, uncritically believes what he or she is told, including illogical conclusions, propaganda, and slogans. In the intellectual realm, too, what reinforces children's natural heteronomy, thereby hindering the development of autonomy, is reward and punishment. What fosters the development of autonomy in the intellectual realm, too, is the exchange of points of view, as we saw in Chapter 3. We saw in that chapter that a nonconserver can make intellectual advances by critically exchanging ideas with another person who has a different but equally erroneous idea.

Unfortunately, in math education, most children are taught in ways that reinforce their heteronomy. For example, if a first grader writes "8" under the problem shown below, most teachers mark this answer as being wrong. If, on the other hand, a first grader writes "26," most teachers give some sort of "reinforcement."

$$13$$
$$+\ 13$$

As was pointed out in Chapter 2, first graders do not understand place value and think that the 1 in 13 means *one*. If they are taught to write "26" and to read it as "twenty-six," therefore, they do not understand why this answer is correct. For them, this problem is two separate problems—3 + 3 and 1 + 1. They follow the rule of writing two answers vertically in the designated spots, and of reading the numbers horizontally to make one answer out of two.

For the reader who is skeptical about the preceding argument, let us give another example, this one using the following computation in division:

$$4\overline{)938}^{\,2}$$

If the reader asks any fourth grader why he or she begins on the lefthand side, instead of beginning on the righthand side as in adding, subtracting, or multiplying multidigit numbers, the answer is likely to be, "I don't know why, but the teacher told me to do it like this." This is an example of intellectual heteronomy. Blindly following rules to get "right" answers reinforces young children's natural heteronomy and hinders the development of autonomy.

To return to the addition problem given earlier, 13 + 13, it would be much better for the teacher to encourage the exchange of viewpoints among children than to reinforce "right" answers or to correct "wrong" ones. A way to encourage the exchange of viewpoints is to ask the class, "Does everybody agree?" In this situation, the children who got the "right" answer would not be able to convince others by saying, "The teacher said to do it this way." Those who got incorrect answers will correct themselves if and when they become convinced that another answer makes better sense. In the logico-mathematical realm, children are bound to arrive at the truth autonomously if they debate long enough.

AUTONOMY AS THE AIM OF EDUCATION

The reader may have concluded by now that autonomy as the aim of education is a necessary consequence of constructivism. Specific moral rules, as well as bits of information, can be acquired by *internalization* from the environment, but deep moral convictions and logico-mathematical knowledge must be *constructed* from the inside. Once we understand the difference between the morality of autonomy and the morality of heteronomy, we become convinced of the desirability of the former. Once we understand the superiority of intellectual autonomy, we likewise become convinced of the desirability of independent, honest, and critical thinking rather than the recitation of "right" answers.

Figure 4.1 shows the relationship between autonomy as the aim of education and the goals of most educators and the public today. We wanted to put the label "Heteronomy" on the circle to the right but did not because most educators today have not heard of autonomy and heteronomy and do not *intentionally* try to foster heteronomy in their students.

In the shaded part of the circle to the right belong all the words we memorized in school just to pass one test after another. We all remember the joy of being free to forget the words we crammed into our heads just for

Figure 4.1. Autonomy as the aim of education, in relation to the goals of most educators and the public.

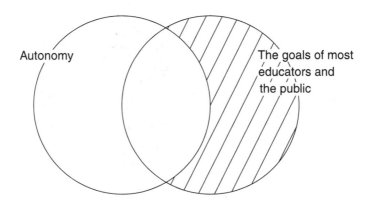

exams. Most of us were conformists, governed by grades. Included in the shaded part of Figure 4.1 are also the rules and algorithms we blindly followed in math to get "right" answers. Kindergarten children do not grab their erasers when we ask them how they got an answer. In first grade, by contrast, if we select a correct answer on a worksheet a child is filling out and ask, "How did you get this answer?" the child often starts erasing the answer. This is a symptom of heteronomy. This child has learned to distrust his or her own thinking and to be governed by someone else's thinking.

In the circle labeled "Autonomy" we include both moral and intellectual autonomy. In his discussion of autonomy as the aim of education, Piaget (1948/1973) selected math education as an example to argue that, in the reality of a classroom, children's social, moral, and intellectual development are inseparable. His argument began with the statement that all children must do their own thinking autonomously to construct logico-mathematical knowledge. In the logico-mathematical realm, there is no substitute for each child's own thinking, because this knowledge has to be constructed from within. Piaget went on to say that children's thinking develops in a social context. Every classroom has a social climate, and this climate cannot encourage the free exchange of viewpoints in the intellectual realm while stifling it in the sociomoral realm. If children are silenced in the sociomoral realm, they will not feel free to express their ideas in the intellectual realm either.

In the overlapping part of the two circles in Figure 4.1, we put the little bit of autonomy we developed in spite of traditional, authoritarian schooling. Our ability to read, write, and do some math are examples of the things we learned in school that we did not forget after the examinations. Other examples of things that belong to this intersection are our ability to put some events in historical context, to read maps and charts, and to understand a few things scientifically.

A principle of teaching that flows from autonomy as the aim of education is the reduction of the teacher's power *as much as possible* and the fostering of self-government (democracy). When children are allowed to make decisions, they often make the same rules that adults would make, but they respect the rules they themselves make much more than the same rules imposed by adults.

An example of the inseparability of the many aspects of autonomy can be seen when children play math games. Children cannot benefit from math games if they are constantly bickering or cheating, and games can become a context for children to learn how to make rules for themselves. When children are given worksheets, the teacher makes all the decisions about what to do and which answer is correct. When they play math games, by contrast, they can learn to make decisions for themselves about what is fair, which answer is correct, and whether or not it makes sense to change a rule.

Attitudes improve greatly when our aim is autonomy. Children become excited and proud of the ideas they have thought about and become confident in their own ability to think. For example, by the end of the school year, our second graders matter-of-factly tackle problems like 46×18 (by doing $46 + 46 + 46 + \ldots$). By contrast, traditionally instructed second graders usually do not even try to think, and say, "We haven't had this kind."

It is often said that school is for the intellect, and that moral education belongs to the home. We hope we have clarified the statement made earlier that moral education goes on during every moment of the school day whether or not we are aware of this fact. Some children occasionally break into tears when we encourage them to disagree with each other. If the teacher reacts by asking the class what *we* can do about this problem, children learn to take relevant factors into account and make positive suggestions. When children are encouraged to exchange viewpoints in this way, they construct from within the rule of showing consideration for others. Sociomoral and intellectual education thus proceed inseparably during every moment in school.

Children who are brought up to feel responsible for the welfare of others, do not cause the kind of shooting incident that happened in Columbine. Empiricist educators try to solve one problem after another with metal detectors and programs for conflict resolution, drug prevention, AIDS prevention, and so on. True reform would address the larger, underlying problem, which is children's heteronomy.

Autonomy as the aim of education is a vast subject we could go on discussing, but let us go on to the next chapter on objectives for second-grade arithmetic.

CHAPTER 5

Objectives for Second-Grade Arithmetic

FOR SOME PEOPLE, "arithmetic" means computation, which can be mindless, and "mathematics" refers to reasoning. For us, however, the two major parts of mathematics are numerical reasoning, or arithmetic, which leads to algebra, and spatial reasoning, which leads to geometry. It is for this reason that we use the term "arithmetic" in the title of this book and this chapter.

The objectives discussed in this chapter are based on our experience with second graders in two public schools in middle- to upper-middle-class neighborhoods. We hasten to say, therefore, that these objectives may or may not be appropriate for second graders in other schools. When we believe that children construct their own logico-mathematical knowledge, we cannot define objectives for second graders and expect all of them to reach these objectives. If children are taught to "carry" and to "borrow," most of them learn to produce correct answers (albeit without understanding). When they are expected to invent their own procedures, however, some second graders demand four-digit addition problems by the end of second grade, while a few remain unable to construct *tens*. Individual differences are thus considerable, and constructivist teaching cannot take place by following a recipe.

We first will discuss our goals for addition and then go on to multiplication, division, and subtraction. The reason for this sequence is that, for second graders, subtraction seems to be the most difficult of the four operations. In fact, the kind of subtraction that requires "borrowing" seems difficult even for many fourth and fifth graders.

ADDITION

Addition of Single-Digit Numbers

As stated in *Young Children Reinvent Arithmetic* (Kamii, 2000), our goal in single-digit addition in first grade is that children construct a network of numerical relationships. Part of such a network is illustrated in Figure 5.1. This goal is different from that of merely getting children to know independent "addition facts." Constructing a network of numerical relationships means that we want children to think about "seven," for example, in all the different, interrelated ways, such as $3 + 4 = 7$, $(3 + 3) + 1 = 7$, $(5 + 4) - 2 = 7$, and $7 =$ half of 14. The child who has constructed this kind of network in his or her mind can use it to change $7 + 8$, for example, to $(7 + 7) + 1$, to $(7 + 3) + 5$, or to $(8 + 2) + 5$. A network of numerical relationships will serve the child throughout life in all the other mathematical operations as well.

In second grade, our goal for single-digit addition is fluency. Some children already have fluency in first grade, but many especially need to learn the "doubles" greater than $6 + 6$ and the harder combinations that make 10, that is, $4 + 6$ and $7 + 3$. These are important not only in themselves but also for adding larger single-digit numbers. To do $8 + 6$, for example, knowing $8 + 2 = 10$ enables children to change the problem to $(8 + 2) + 4$. Knowing $6 + 6 = 12$ likewise enables them to change the problem to $(6 + 6) + 2$. Furthermore, as we will see toward the end of this chapter, fluency in single-digit addition enables children to become fluent in subtraction.

Addition of Multidigit Numbers

First Goal. The first goal in two-digit addition is for children to invent ways of adding single-digit numbers that involve making 10. As can be seen in the videotape entitled *Double-Column Addition* (Kamii, 1989a), problems such as $9 + 6$ are especially useful because they motivate children to think *simultaneously* about *ones* $(9 + 1 + 5)$ and a *ten* $(10 + 5)$, thereby fostering the construction of "one ten" out of the system of ones. Similar examples are $8 + 5$ and $7 + 4$.

Second Goal. The next goal is that children invent ways of adding addends up to 19 in problems such as $13 + 6$, $18 + 5$, $13 + 13$, and $15 + 16$. Note that children have to deal with tens and ones *simultaneously* in various contexts to solve these problems. Traditional textbooks give two-digit addition problems without regrouping in first grade and wait a long time to present problems with regrouping in second grade. By contrast, we give the preceding four kinds of problems almost at the same time. Our reason is that we want children to invent *tens* in many contexts, out of their system of *ones*. Giving nothing but problems like $13 + 13$ day after day is a sure way of encouraging them *not* to think about tens and ones *simultaneously*.

Figure 5.1. An example of the network of numerical relationships.

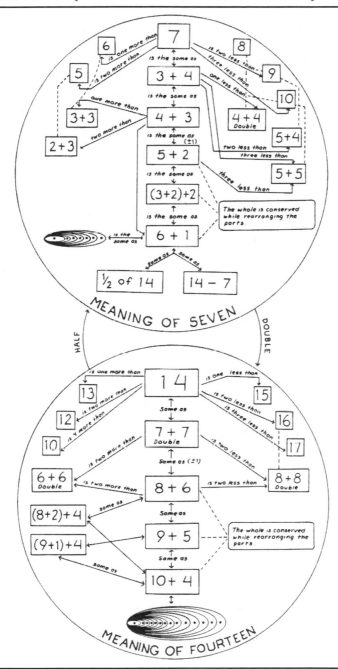

We need to spend a long time giving two-digit numbers that are small enough to make intuitive sense. In the task involving 48 lima beans described in Chapter 2, Ross (1986) went on to empty one of the four cups in front of the child and asked whether the total number was still the same or whether there were more now or more before she emptied one cup (leaving three cups each containing 10 beans and 18 loose ones). Only 33% of the second graders answered that the number of beans remained the same. This finding indicates that, for two-thirds of the second graders, conservation was possible with eight objects but not with 48. For them, 48 was a huge number.

Third Goal. Our third goal is for children to invent ways of adding addends up to 99 (and then three- and four-digit addends, if appropriate). It is sometimes easy to judge the right time to go on to harder problems because children demand them. They are so excited about being able to invent clever procedures that they often say, "That's too easy! Give us a harder one!"

Place Value

Knowledge of place value is obviously very important, but, as stated in Chapter 2, we do not provide specific activities just to teach place value and do not conceptualize place value as a separate goal. We saw earlier that part of our goal in giving addition problems (as well as multiplication and division problems) is to foster children's knowledge of place value. In other words, we transmit the social knowledge of place value through use, when this knowledge is useful to children.

With a problem like 9 + 6 written vertically on the board, for example, a volunteer may begin by saying, "I know that 9 and 1 is 10." The teacher may then erase the "9" and write "10" and then "– 1 = 5" to the right of the "6." As the child proceeds to say "10 + 5 = 15," the teacher erases the "0" of "10," writes "5" in its place, and erases everything except the answer 15. This writing is useful for three reasons. First, it is useful to the volunteer because it communicates that the teacher understood his or her reasoning. Second, it is useful to the rest of the class because it serves to clarify the volunteer's statements and permits other students to ask a question if something does not make sense. It is useful to all the students also because they can see how place value works as the teacher writes and erases numbers.

In our opinion, this is the best way to "teach" place value without teaching it directly in isolation. In the preceding situation, children are free to concentrate on the construction of *tens* out of their own system of *ones*, which is the hardest part of double-digit addition for second graders. When this logico-mathematical knowledge is solid, the social knowledge of place value comes easily through use.

MULTIPLICATION

Subtraction is usually considered to be easier than multiplication, but we find that multiplication is easier for second graders, especially in the form of word problems. The reason is that children in kindergarten and grades 1 and 2 use repeated addition instead of multiplication (Kamii, 2000). In second grade, an increasing number of students begin to use some multiplication. Let us explain the difference between repeated addition and multiplication.

Additive and Multiplicative Thinking

For most mathematics educators, multiplication is only a faster way of doing repeated addition. For researchers such as Piaget (1983/1987), Steffe (1988, 1992), and Clark and Kamii (1996), however, multiplication is different from repeated addition because it involves hierarchical thinking. As can be seen in Figure 5.2(a), the structure of repeated addition such as 5 + 5 + 5 + 5 is simple because it involves only *ones* at one level of abstraction. Multiplication such as 4 × 5 involves the hierarchical structure shown in Figure 5.2(b). It can be seen in this figure that the "4" in 4 × 5 refers to "4 fives." To read "4 × 5" correctly, the child has to be able to transform "5 *ones*" into "one *five*," which is a higher-order unit. In other words, in "4 × 5," the "4" is not the same kind of number as the "5."

Clark and Kamii (1996) interviewed 336 students in grades 1–5 in a public school serving a middle-income neighborhood. As reported in Kamii (2000), they found four levels that clearly differentiated between multiplicative and additive thinkers (see Table 5.1). The additive thinkers understood "two times" and "three times" to mean "2 more [than 4, for

Figure 5.2. The difference between (a) repeated addition and (b) multiplication.

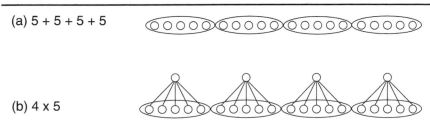

(a) 5 + 5 + 5 + 5

(b) 4 x 5

Table 5.1: Number and Percentage of Children at Each Developmental Level by Grade

Level	Grade				
	1	2	3	4	5
1 [a]	8 (13.8)	1 (1.5)	—	—	—
2 [b]	31 (53.4)	28 (43.1)	8 (13.6)	12 (15.4)	5 (6.6)
3 [b]	8 (13.8)	7 (10.8)	13 (22.0)	2 (2.6)	2 (2.6)
4A [c]	10 (17.2)	23 (35.4)	25 (42.4)	42 (53.8)	32 (42.1)
4B [c]	1 (1.7)	6 (9.2)	13 (22.0)	22 (28.2)	37 (48.7)
Total	58 (99.9)	65 (100)	59 (100)	78 (100)	76 (100)

Note: Values enclosed in parentheses represent percentages.

[a] Below additive

[b] Additive

[c] Multiplicative

From "Identification of Multiplicative Thinking in Children in Grades 1–5," by F. B. Clark and C. Kamii, 1996, *Journal for Research in Mathematics Education*, 27, p. 48. Copyright © 1996 by National Council of Teacher of Mathematics. Reprinted with permission.

example]" and "3 more," even after a demonstration of what "two times" and "three times" meant. Children cannot understand logico-mathematical relationships that they are not yet able to make in their heads.

On the basis of the data in Table 5.1, we conclude that we can expect more than half of the second graders to solve "multiplication" word problems with repeated addition but not with multiplication. The majority of second graders understand "five packages of gum each containing six pieces of gum" as 6 + 6 + 6 + 6 + 6 and not as 5 × 6.

Our Goal in Multiplication

Our goal in multiplication is that children invent ways of solving word problems that traditionally are thought to be multiplication problems. Those who can think multiplicatively can use multiplication, and those who cannot can use repeated addition to solve these problems.

Traditional textbooks give computational problems first and introduce word problems afterwards so children can *apply* computational skills to the word problems. By contrast, in an approach based on Piaget's constructivism, we give word problems first so that children will *logico-arithmetize* the situation and *invent* computational procedures to solve the problems. Historically, our ancestors invented arithmetic to solve practical problems, and arithmetic is the logico-arithmetization of contents such as sheep. Children, too, invent arithmetic by solving practical problems in real life or in situations resembling real life.

In November, one of us (LJ) gave a problem like, "Let's pretend that Adam, Brad, Cindy, and Dana (pointing to four people in the class) each have eight stickers. How many stickers would there be all together?" Many of the children doubled eight and doubled the double ($8 + 8 = 16$ and $16 + 16 = 32$).

The numbers became larger as the year progressed. An example is: There are 21 children here today. How much money would I collect if everybody ordered a pencil with his or her name on it, and each cost 46 cents? Most of the children got the answer by writing "46" 21 times and laboriously using addition. Some got the total for ten 46s, doubled the total, and added 46.

Traditional second-grade textbooks present double-column addition (with regrouping) early in the school year and multiplication of small numbers toward the end of the year. By contrast, we present "multiplication" word problems with small numbers in kindergarten and continue to give word problems involving all four operations throughout the year. We also give two-step problems such as those asking how much change to expect from 50 cents if one wanted to buy several objects at a certain price.

"Friendly" combinations such as 3×25 (cents) $= 75$, $4 \times 3 = 12$, and $4 \times 5 = 20$ become part of children's repertoires as they count money and play games repeatedly. Note that our objective in second grade is neither that they know the multiplication tables nor that they become able to write equations correctly. Our objective is that children *think* about the problem and figure out the answer in whatever way they can. We push multiplication from time to time by asking for a faster way, giving "friendly" numbers, or calling on children who are using multiplication. But we never say that children *have to* use multiplication.

DIVISION

Our goal in division is very similar to what we said about multiplication. Most children use repeated addition to solve "division" problems, and more and more begin to use some multiplication as the year progresses.

One day, a mother gave one of us (LJ) a check for $5.75 for her child's birthday celebration, to get popsicles for everybody in the class. Knowing that this was a fourth-grade problem, Linda hesitated but decided to take a chance. "I have to know *right now* if 5 dollars and 75 cents is enough to get a popsicle for everybody who is here today because either everybody gets one, or nobody will get one," she announced. Everybody knew that the cafeteria sold popsicles for 25 cents.

Most of the children counted four members of the class and said, "That's one dollar." They counted four more members and said, "That's two dollars." They continued to 3, 4, and 5 dollars as they counted four more children each time. There were two children and the teacher left at the end, and everybody agreed that there was exactly the right amount of money to get a popsicle for everybody.

We were very impressed by the children's resourcefulness. The only limitations are the size of the dividend and the "friendliness" of the divisor. With 25 cents as the divisor, children are willing to deal with larger dividends. The reader may have seen the videotape made in one of our schools entitled "First Graders Dividing 62 by 5" (Kamii & Clark, 2000) and may know that divisors such as 2, 5, 10, 11, and 25 are much easier than 3 and 4.

The popsicle problem was a quotitive division problem. In giving word problems to children, we make sure that children get both quotitive and partitive division problems. An example of a partitive division problem is: How much would each person get if 22 people were to divide $5.75? In a partitive division problem, the number of parts into which the total has to be divided is known.

Another point to remember is to give problems with numbers that are divisible as well as those that are not exactly divisible. Traditional textbooks give only divisible numbers for a long time, such as 18 to be divided by 6, and many children say that 17 cannot be divided by 6. As the title of the videotape "First Graders Dividing 62 by 5" (Kamii & Clark, 2000) implies, our first graders deal with remainders from the beginning. Children need to figure out that money left over after buying erasers can be a remainder, but that when a game can be played by a maximum of three people, and there are 22 children in the class, "seven with a remainder of one" is not a satisfactory answer (because leaving one child out would be an injustice).

Fractions

As stated in *Young Children Reinvent Arithmetic* (Kamii, 2000), Empson (1995) found that before any instruction, 14 out of a class of 17 first graders solved the problem of four children sharing 10 cupcakes equally. Thirds were more difficult than halves and repeated halving. Empson's work is part of a program called Cognitively Guided Instruction (Carpenter, Fennema, Franke, Levi, & Empson, 1999), in which children invent arithmetic through word problems. The teacher does not show the students how to solve the problems and, instead, encourages them to come up with their own procedures and to exchange viewpoints about what they have done and why. To encourage second graders to invent common fractions like 1/3 and 1/4, the teacher may give problems such as dividing seven candy bars among three children, nine cupcakes among four children, and eight pancakes among six children.

SUBTRACTION

All the textbooks we know, as well as *Principles and Standards for School Mathematics* (National Council of Teachers of Mathematics, 2000), treat subtraction as if it were at the same difficulty level as addition. Piaget (1974/1980a) showed, however, that a characteristic of infancy and early childhood is the general primacy of the positive aspect of actions, perception, and cognition over the negative aspect. For example, when toddlers look at a red ball, they first think positively about it as "a ball" and "red" and later become able to think about it negatively as "*not* a doll," "*not* an apple," and "*not* blue." Similarly, when they walk from A to B, they think positively about walking toward B rather than away from A. The negative aspect is a later, secondary construction, according to Piaget, and he supported this statement with two volumes of empirical studies. In this context, he pointed out that subtraction is a secondary development that appears after addition.

Based on this theory and observations in classrooms, Kamii, Lewis, and Kirkland (2001) hypothesized that differences must appear after sums because children produce differences by deduction from their knowledge of sums. More specifically, they decided to ask children to solve related addition and subtraction problems such as 4 + 4 and 8 – 4. If fluency in subtraction was found to be unrelated to fluency in addition, it would be concluded that knowledge of differences is independent of knowledge of sums. If, on the other hand, fluency in subtraction was found to depend on fluency in addition, the conclusion would be that differences are deduced from knowledge of sums. This study is reviewed below, even though it did not involve second graders, because it explains why we believe that the way to increase fluency in subtraction is to strengthen children's knowledge of sums.

Kamii, Lewis, and Kirkland's (2001) Study

Method. Twenty-one first graders from one class and 38 fourth graders from two classes were interviewed individually in a constructivist "school within a school" in a middle- to upper-middle-class neighborhood. The children in this school had never been pressured to memorize sums or differences. They played many math games and invented many ways of solving problems, but were not given any worksheet or timed test. The first graders were interviewed at the end of the school year, and the fourth graders were seen at the beginning of the year.

The interviews were part of the routine assessment conducted at the beginning and end of the school year with a four-page form. The form contained about 70 one-, two-, and three-digit computational problems involving all four operations. Both the child and the adult had a copy of the form that had the questions in a column on the lefthand side. The child was asked to give the answer to each question orally and to slide a ruler down to the next question. The interviewer recorded what the child said and from time to time asked for an explanation of how an answer was obtained. One dot per second was recorded to show the child's reaction time.

Only two of the four pages of the interview form were used with the first graders. The fourth graders were told that they could say, "I want to skip it" if a problem was too hard. The children were not told that speed mattered in this assessment.

For this study, four pairs of questions were selected from the first graders' interviews: $4 + 4$ and $8 - 4$, $6 + 6$ and $12 - 6$, $8 + 2$ and $10 - 8$, and $4 + 6$ and $10 - 6$. All the addition problems appeared at the beginning of the interview, and the subtraction problems came toward the end.

New questions were added to the form for the fourth graders to make eight pairs of problems: Three of the eight pairs were the same as those given to the first graders, but the following five were added: $5 + 3$ and $8 - 5$, $5 + 6$ and $11 - 5$, $7 + 4$ and $11 - 4$, $7 + 8$ and $15 - 8$, and $8 + 5$ and $13 - 5$.

The children's responses were dichotomized into "successful" and "unsuccessful" categories. To be included in the "successful" category, the child had to give the correct answer within 3 seconds. All other responses were considered "unsuccessful." Most of the children in the "unsuccessful" category produced correct answers but took more than 3 seconds to think or to count.

Findings. The results for $4 + 4$ and $8 - 4$ given to first graders are presented in Figure 5.3(a). It can be seen from this matrix that addition was easier than subtraction, as all the first graders ($67\% + 33\%$) produced the correct answer to $4 + 4$ within 3 seconds, but only 67% were successful in $8 - 4$. The more important comparison is between the upper lefthand cell and the lower righthand cell. It can be seen in these cells that 33% were successful in addition but not in subtraction, but no one was successful in subtraction without being successful in addition.

Figure 5.3. Percentage of first and fourth graders responding successfully and unsuccessfully to related addition and subtraction problems.

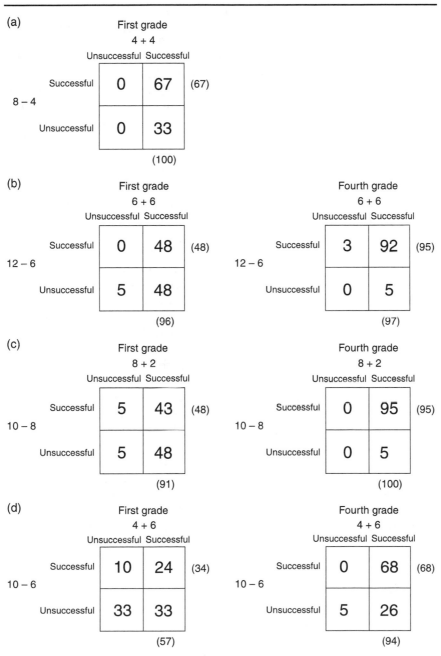

Figure 5.3(b) presents results for 6 + 6 and 12 − 6. The same pattern can be observed in first grade, with 48% being successful in addition but not in subtraction, and no one succeeding in subtraction without being successful in addition. In fourth grade, the percentage successful in 6 + 6 is the same as in first grade (48% + 48% vs. 92% + 5%). However, the percentage successful in 12 − 6 increased dramatically to 95% (3% + 92%) in fourth grade. This increase shows that when knowledge of 6 + 6 is very solid by fourth grade, fluency in subtraction greatly improves. Figure 5.3(c), showing results for 8 + 2 and 10 − 8, leads to the same conclusion because the percentages are almost identical to those in Figure 5.3(b).

The most important cell to focus on in the four matrices in Figures 5.3(b) and 5.3(c) is the upper lefthand cell. We can see that it is impossible or almost impossible, both in first grade and in fourth grade, to be fluent in 12 − 6 without being fluent in 6 + 6, and to be fluent in 10 − 8 without being fluent in 8 + 2. The 3% in fourth grade represents one child who was categorized as being unsuccessful in 6 + 6 because he was not paying attention and took more than 3 seconds to give the correct answer. The 5% in first grade represents one child who was inattentive when asked about 8 + 2.

Figure 5.3(d), presenting results for 4 + 6 and 10 − 6, concerns addends that are harder for first graders. The percentages for first graders are different from those in the rest of Figure 5.3 in that a large percentage, 33%, were unsuccessful both in addition and subtraction. This matrix, as well as the one for fourth graders, nevertheless shows again that it is almost impossible to be successful in subtraction without being successful in addition. The 10% represents 2 out of 21 children who were not concentrating on the task.

Figure 5.4 shows the percentages for the fourth graders, who were given harder questions. If we examine the upper lefthand cells of all five matrices in Figure 5.4, we note again that the percentages in those cells are zero or close to zero. (One of the five cells has 11%, but 11% is only 4 out of 38 students.) The data in Figures 5.3 and 5.4 thus led Kamii and colleagues (2001) to conclude that children *deduce* differences from their knowledge of sums. This theory is different from the one that states that children *store* and *retrieve* "subtraction facts," like computers. According to Piaget (Piaget & Inhelder, 1968/1973), memory cannot be explained as mere storage and retrieval because it is the reconstruction of previous constructions.

Goals for Single-Digit Subtraction

Our goal in single-digit subtraction is fluency, but, for the reasons given above, we restate this goal and say that we strengthen children's knowl-

Figure 5.4. Percentage of fourth graders responding successfully and unsuccessfully to related addition and subtraction problems.

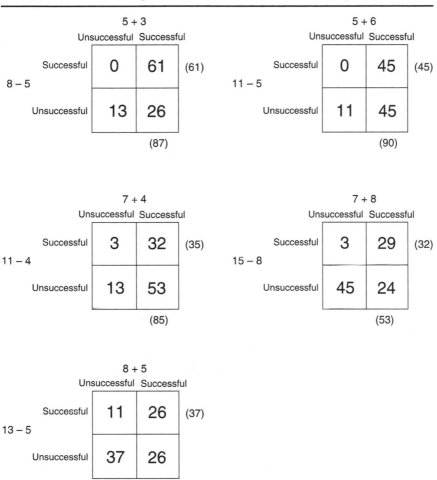

edge of sums so that they will become able to deduce differences from their knowledge of sums. We therefore provide many games that require addition and de-emphasize subtraction in second grade.

As can be seen in Figure 5.5(a), addition is easy for young children because in 5 + 4, for example, they have only to "ascend" from a lower level to a hierarchically higher level. By contrast, 9 – 5 is hard because children have to "descend" from 9 to 5 and "ascend" back to 9 (the whole)

Figure 5.5. The difference in thinking between (a) addition and (b) subtraction.

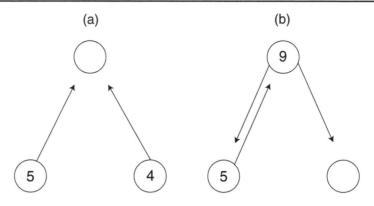

before "descending" to the other part. In this final descent, children who know 5 + 4 = 9 have an advantage over those who do not know this sum.

Goals for Two-Digit Subtraction

As can be seen in the videotape *Double-Column Addition* (Kamii, 1989a), many second graders invent one of the following three ways of dealing with problems like 26 – 17.

20 – 10 = 10	20 – 10 = 10	20 – 10 = 10
10 + 6 = 16	10 – 7 = 3	6 – 7 = –1
16 – 7 = 9	3 + 6 = 9	10 – 1 = 9

We subsequently learned that this kind of problem is hard even for some fourth and fifth graders. It is therefore reasonable to expect two-digit subtraction in second grade from those who can do it, but we must remember that this is too hard for some second graders, even if they have constructed a system of *tens*. We can think of three reasons for this difficulty.

First, even with single-digit numbers, subtraction is much harder than addition, as we saw in Figure 5.5. Second, two-digit subtraction requires making too many part–whole relationships for second graders to remember. To do 26 – 17, for example, children have to remember the following five part–whole relationships: (a) 17 is part of 26, (b) 20 is part of 26, (c) 6 is part of 26, (d) 10 is part of 17, and (e) 7 is part of 17. The common error of 26 – 17 = 11 is made by children who cannot remember that 17 is part of 26, that 6 is part of 26, and that 7 is part of 17.

Third, two-digit subtraction requires the ability to think *simultaneously* about addition and subtraction, when it is hard enough for second graders to think only about subtraction. In doing 26 – 17, for example, 20 – 10 = 10 is usually easy. However, children who then do 10 + 6 do this *with the intention of subtracting 7 afterwards*. It is this simultaneous thinking about addition and subtraction that is hard for many second graders, and these children cannot understand the need to use addition when 26 – 17 is a subtraction problem. (Some children do 20 – 10 = 10, and then 10 – 7 *with the intention of adding 6 afterwards*. The difficulty of having to think simultaneously about addition and subtraction is exactly the same.)

CONCLUSION

In conclusion, our goals and objectives for second-grade arithmetic include all four of the operations, with heavy emphasis on addition. Our reasons for emphasizing addition are that (a) most second graders are additive rather than multiplicative thinkers, and (b) ability to subtract depends on knowledge of sums and ability to think simultaneously about addition and subtraction. As far as the magnitude of numbers is concerned, we make sure that children can deal solidly with numbers up to 20. We then gradually increase the numbers if children seem willing and eager to deal with them. If they seem unsure, we go back to easier numbers.

We emphasize word problems so that computation will grow out of the need to solve word problems. Place value is also taught in this context. Children who invent their own procedures for multidigit operations struggle to solve problems. But this struggle brings joy, confidence, and excitement to them, which are in sharp contrast to the emotional flatness we observe when children are taught to "carry" and to "borrow."

PART III

Activities

CHAPTER 6

Discussions of Computational and Story Problems

with Linda Joseph

MANY TEACHERS ASK, "What do you do to get children to invent arithmetic after throwing out the textbook and workbook?" Our answer is that we use three kinds of activities—(1) teacher-initiated discussions of computational and story problems, (2) discussions about situations in daily living (e.g., figuring out, as we saw in Chapter 5, whether $5.75 is enough to buy a popsicle for every member of the class), and (3) math games. This chapter is devoted to the first kind of activity, teacher-initiated discussions. In Chapter 7, Linda Joseph describes the use of situations in daily living and other activities. Math games are then presented in Chapter 8.

Ways of adding two-digit numbers are hard for most second graders to invent, even when regrouping is not required. This is why the teacher takes the initiative to present the right kind of problem at the right time, depending on where children are in their development of numerical reasoning. Generally, about half of the math hour is spent on these discussions and the other half on games.

Because our principles of teaching are very different from the traditional ones teachers follow, we discuss them first. These principles and theoretical rationale are important to understand because our way of teaching depends on the teacher's assessment of how children are thinking from moment to moment. In other words, our way of teaching cannot be reduced to recipes or a teacher's guide specifying what to do from one day to the next. We then discuss our general sequence of objectives as the teacher thinks about them in practice, and conclude with examples of math hours that took place in October, February, and May.

In this chapter, we devote more space to computational problems than to story problems because the latter are similar to the situations described in Chapter 7. The teacher invents story problems based on the operation(s) and magnitude of numbers he or she wants to exercise, using holidays that are approaching (e.g., buying hotdog buns for the Fourth of July), topics that come up in other areas of the curriculum (e.g., the number of legs on many flies and spiders), and what children spontaneously talk about.

PRINCIPLES OF TEACHING

Five principles are listed first, and each is then explained.

1. Start with word problems, and let computation develop out of word problems.
2. Do not show children how to solve problems; instead, encourage them to invent their own procedures.
3. Refrain from reinforcing correct answers and correcting wrong ones, and, instead, encourage the exchange of points of view among children. (The correct answer always surfaces.)
4. Encourage children to invent many different ways of solving a problem.
5. Encourage children to *think* rather than to write; write on the chalkboard to (a) facilitate the exchange of viewpoints and (b) teach place value.

Starting with Word Problems

In traditional instruction, children are taught computational techniques first and then given word problems so they can *apply* these techniques. According to Piaget's constructivism, as stated in Chapter 5, our ancestors constructed arithmetic out of the practical problems they encountered. Today's children, too, can construct arithmetic as they try to figure out how many chairs to set up, how many cookies each person should take, and so on. This numerical thinking in real-life situations is an example of what Piaget called "the logico-arithmetization of reality." We start by giving word problems so that children will have opportunities to logico-arithmetize situations that resemble real life. For example, if there are four children at a table, and each child is to get five cookies, children have to decide whether to do 4 + 5, 5 + 5 + 5 + 5, or something else to figure out how many cookies are needed. This is the "logic" part of logico-arithmetization. The numerical reasoning involved in getting the exact answer is the "arithmetic" part.

Encouraging Children to Invent Their Own Procedures

Traditional math educators do not make a distinction between logico-mathematical knowledge and social-conventional knowledge, and assume that mathematics has to be socially transmitted to children. In other words, they assume that children do not know how to add 15 and 17, for example, unless they are taught how to do this. As explained in Chapter 1, however, children construct number from within and can figure out how to operate on numbers that *they* have created.

The reader may be wondering what the teacher can do if children cannot invent a solution. Children always use what they already know to invent new procedures. Therefore, one way to make an invention possible is to give smaller numbers and/or friendly numbers. For example, if dividing 27 M&M's among four children is too hard, the teacher might change the problem to an easier one: dividing 15 among five children, or 12 among three children. Another technique is to ask questions such as, "Would it help to make a drawing (or use pretend M&M's)?" or "Would it help to read the question again?" (followed by, "What is the question asking for?").

Encouraging the Exchange of Viewpoints

In traditional instruction, one of the teacher's major responsibilities is to reinforce correct answers and correct wrong ones. Children thus learn to be afraid of being wrong and begin to read the teacher's face to know whether or not she looks pleased. Furthermore, all thinking stops when the teacher announces that an answer is correct.

Instead of saying, "That's right," or "That's wrong," we stimulate the exchange of viewpoints by asking, "Does everybody agree?" The exchange of points of view among children is very important for us, as shown in Chapter 3. Mathematics did not develop historically through reinforcement by a higher authority. Each invention was supported or rejected by debate among peers. In a classroom, too, if everybody agrees that an argument makes sense, children can conclude for themselves that an answer is correct. If children realize that somebody else's argument makes better sense, they are perfectly willing to correct themselves *from within*, without any pressure.

Encouraging Children to Invent Many Different Ways of Solving a Problem

Traditional instruction teaches "*the* one correct way" of dealing with each kind of problem, but children who are encouraged to do their own thinking invent many different ways. To do 15 + 17, for example, one child may do 10 + 10 = 20, 5 + 5 = another ten, 20 + 10 = 30, and 30 + 2 = 32. Another child may do 10 + 10 = 20, 5 + 7 = 12, 20 + 10 = 30, and 30 + 2 = 32. Children who critically evaluate all the different ways their peers have invented, have opportunities to build a complex network of numerical relationships, out of which they will construct an even more elaborate structure.

Encouraging Children to Think, Rather Than to Write

Traditional instruction teaches conventional algorithms, which are rules about where to write numerals and in what order. As can be seen in the videotape *Double-Column Addition* (Kamii, 1989a), writing in our classrooms is what the teacher does, for two main purposes: to facilitate the exchange of viewpoints among children and to teach the social-conventional knowledge of place value.

Back in 1984, when we started to work together, it was clear to us that children should not write anything and should concentrate on thinking, listening, and speaking. We knew of only one person who was saying then that children "universally proceed from left to right" (Madell, 1985, p. 21). Madell made the following statements with respect to

$$36$$
$$+\,46\,.$$

Invariably, in a problem like this, the seven- and eight-year-olds first compute the tens. The details vary:

a) Some will actually record a 7 in the tens column before looking at the ones. These children then come back and erase.

b) Others, having arrived at 7 as the sum of 3 and 4, do not record that 7 before checking the ones column to see if it contains another ten.

c) A few of the most sophisticated students check the ones first. Noting (often by estimation) that there are more than 10 ones in the ones column, they come back to sum the tens and record 8 before returning to the ones and the last detail of the computation. (p. 21)

While Madell's statements were enormously helpful, it seemed to us that the writing and erasing he described showed children's preoccupation with writing. He also spoke about "the sum of 3 and 4" (rather than the sum of 30 and 40), and our children would exclaim "Disagree!" in this situation. If no one disagreed, the teacher would challenge by saying, "I get 19 if I add 3 and 4 and 6 and 6. How did you get 82?"

Below is an example of how the teacher may write and erase as children talk about their thinking. All the desks are cleared before the discussion, and the teacher puts a problem with addends up to 19 on the chalkboard, such as the following:

$$18$$
$$+\ 13$$

He or she then asks, "What's a good way to solve this problem?" It is important for the teacher to take plenty of "wait time," to encourage all the children to think. When most of the hands are up, the teacher calls on individual children and lists all the different answers on the upper lefthand side of board, such as 21, 31, 211, and 13. (Children usually say "Agree!" or "Disagree!" as the teacher writes each answer, but the teacher encourages children not to react at this point.)

Being careful not to say that an answer is right or wrong, the teacher then asks for volunteers to explain how they got their answers. (It soon becomes desirable to ask, "Which answer seems unreasonable [or reasonable] to you?" Children become able to say, for example, that the answer of 13 is unreasonable because one of the addends is 13, or that 211 seems unreasonable because ten-and-something plus ten-and-something cannot possibly be 200.) As a volunteer then explains his or her reasoning, the teacher writes each step on the board and encourages the group to agree or disagree. For example, if a volunteer says, "Ten and 10 is 20," the teacher may point to each 1 (in 18 and 13) and write the child's ideas on the lefthand side as follows:

$$
\begin{array}{cc}
10 & 18 \\
+\ 10 & +\ 13 \\
\hline
20 &
\end{array}
$$

If the child then says, "I take 2 from the 3 and put it with the 8," the teacher points to the 3 and the 8 and writes "−2" and "+2" as follows:

$$
\begin{array}{ccc}
10 & 18 & +2 \\
+\ 10 & +\ 13 & -2 \\
\hline
20 & &
\end{array}
$$

If the child continues with, "That's another 10," the teacher points to the 8 and +2 and writes "10" as shown below:

```
10        18       +2
+ 10     + 13      -2
20
10
```

If the child's next statement is, "Twenty and 10 is 30," the teacher points to the 20 and the 10 below it, erases everything on the lefthand side except the 20, and replaces the 2 with a 3, with the following result:

```
              18       +2
            + 13       -2
30
```

If the child then says, "And 1 more is 31," the teacher points to "3 – 2," erases the 0 of 30, and changes it to 1, with the following result:

```
              18       +2
            + 13       -2
31
```

The teacher then writes "31" under the double-column problem.

The teacher thus erases and writes on the board (a) to let the volunteer know what the teacher understood, and (b) to help the rest of the class follow the explanation. The teacher thus refrains from saying that an argument makes or does not make sense, and encourages the exchange of ideas among children.

The teacher then asks individual children to present all the different ways in which they got the answer. Two other procedures children often invent for the preceding problem are as follows:

$$10 + 10 = 20 \qquad 10 + 10 = 20$$

$$8 + 3 = 11 \qquad 20 + 8 = 28$$

$$20 + 10 = 30 \qquad 28 + 3 = 31$$

$$30 + 1 = 31$$

It is easier at the beginning for children to figure out how place value works if the teacher writes the problem vertically. However, it is also important to present the problem in horizontal form, to avoid creating a dependency on the vertical alignment of columns.

The questions often asked by visitors are: How do you get the discussions started? How do you sequence the problems? and Why do you work with the whole class when everybody else is saying that teachers should work with small groups? These questions will be addressed in the rest of the chapter as Linda Joseph describes some of the activities she used in her class.

GETTING STARTED

The first principle of teaching given earlier was to begin with word problems. This is usually a good idea, but when we want second graders to construct *tens* out of *ones*, which is difficult for most of them, we focus exclusively on numbers. I may begin with a lively game that the entire class plays called Around the World. In this game, two children at a time compete to see who can give the sum of two numbers faster, after I show a flashcard. The first two children stand up to compete. The winner then stands behind (or next to) a third child, and these two wait for me to show the next flashcard. The one who wins then stands behind a fourth child, and so on, until everybody has had a chance to compete. A child who defeats many others and makes it to the end of the line is the champion who is said to have gone "around the world." (The champion usually defeats many other children but not all of them. Before beginning the game, I ask, "Who wants to play Around the World?" because some children are afraid of the competition in this game and should not be forced to compete.)

We play this game for about 30 minutes. I then go to the board and say, "I noticed that Tom answered this question quickly," and write a problem such as the following on the board:

$$\begin{array}{r} 9 \\ + 5 \\ \hline \end{array}$$

"Can anyone think of a fast way to get the answer?" I may ask. One child may say, "You can count it fast in your head," and another may say, "Take 1 off the 5 and put it with the 9." Following the child's statement, I point to the 5 and write "−1," and point to the 9 and write "+1," as shown below, so that everybody can decide whether this procedure makes sense:

$$\begin{array}{rr} 9 & +1 \\ + 5 & -1 \\ \hline \end{array}$$

"That's 10," the child continues, and I add to the computation as follows:

$$
\begin{array}{ll}
9 & +1 = 10 \\
\underline{+\ 5} & -1
\end{array}
$$

As the child says, "And 4 more is 14," I add these numbers as follows:

$$
\begin{array}{ll}
9 & +1 = 10 \\
\underline{+\ 5} & -1 =\ 4 \\
& \quad 14
\end{array}
$$

I may sometimes write much less and follow the same argument by writing only the following:

$$
\begin{array}{ll}
9 & 10 \\
\underline{+\ 5} & 4 \\
14 &
\end{array}
$$

When all alternative procedures have been offered, I go on to another problem such as

$$
\begin{array}{r}
8 \\
\underline{+\ 7}
\end{array}
$$

To this problem, some children respond, "I know 8 and 8 is 16; so take 1 off and it's 15." Others will then agree that doubles are easy, and I encourage them to use what they already know to go on from there. Other ways that children often invent are the following:

$$(7 + 7) + 1$$

$$(8 + 2) + 5$$

$$(7 + 3) + 5$$

After a few days of beginning the math hour by playing Around the World, I stop using this game and go directly to the board and write problems such as the following, one at a time:

$$
\begin{array}{ccc}
5 & 3 & 10 \\
\underline{+\ 3} & \underline{+\ 6} & \underline{+\ 5}
\end{array}
$$

I begin each hour with easy problems with sums up to 10 so that all children have a chance to feel successful. The general sequence I then keep in mind in giving problems is as follows:

1. Single-digit problems, especially those that are likely to suggest the use of doubles, such as 5 + 6, and the use of combinations that make 10, such as 8 + 3.
2. "Ragged-column" problems with "10-plus addends" that do not need regrouping, up to a sum of 19. By "10-plus addends," I mean numbers from 11 to 19. I emphasize them for two reasons: (a) Many second graders can add only ones because for them, 14, for instance, is 14 ones, and not 1 ten and 4 ones, and (b) as pointed out by Ma (1999), it is especially important that children can solidly deal with sums up to 20. Two examples of this category are the following:

$$\begin{array}{ccc} 12 & & 15 \\ + \ 6 & \text{and} & + \ 4 \end{array}$$

3. "Ragged-column" and two-digit problems with "10-plus addends," some of which require regrouping. Examples include the following:

$$\begin{array}{cccc} 16 & 10 & 13 & 19 \\ + \ 4 & + 12 & + 13 & + \ 2 \end{array}$$

During each math hour, I mix problems that require regrouping and those that do not. One of my reasons is that children might otherwise construct the rule (or trick), for example, of merely adding each column as ones. I pay particular attention to combinations that make 10 by giving problems such as 17 + 3 and 12 + 8. I then go on to larger addends such as 36 + 5 and 38 + 13.
4. Problems involving many numbers, such as the following:

$$\begin{array}{c} 7 \\ 4 \\ 8 \\ 3 \\ + 2 \end{array}$$

Again, I pay particular attention to combinations that make 10, such as 7 + 3 and 8 + 2 in the preceding example.

I go as far as the children can go during each hour. The practice of going through a variety of problems during each math hour is in contrast to textbook instruction, which focuses on only one type of exercise each day (such as double-column addition with one regrouping). I prefer to offer a variety partly because children benefit from hearing discussions of problems they think are too hard for them. Almost every day, someone will attempt a new and harder type of problem for the first time, and I am ecstatic when this happens.

I sometimes invite small groups of less advanced children to work on problems with me while others play games. However, I insist on having the entire class for the discussions because the less advanced children sometimes benefit from listening to the more advanced students. They may or may not understand what is being said, but if they are excluded, they are sure *not* to be exposed to higher-level arguments.

One day in mid-September, an advanced child begged for "something harder, something in the hundreds." So I wrote the following problem for him:

$$\begin{array}{r} 73 \\ + 38 \\ \hline \end{array}$$

Amazingly, he gave the correct answer after a brief moment. When I asked how he got his answer, he said he had added 30 to 70 and gotten 100, and 11 more made 111.

I then decided to check the rest of the class for their method of tackling a type of problem they probably had never encountered before. So I wrote this problem on the board:

$$\begin{array}{r} 46 \\ + 46 \\ \hline \end{array}$$

I walked around the room and had the children whisper their answers in my ear, and, without comment, I listed them all on the board: 91, 92, 20, 81, and 812.

After sufficient wait time, I said to the class, "Now I want you to tell me how you reached your answers," and then asked, "Who got this answer?" pointing to the answer of 812. When Katie identified herself, I asked her where she had begun. She said, "Four plus 4 is 8, and 6 plus 6 is 12; so the answer is 812." I asked the class if they agreed, and many exclaimed that they did not. "Why not?" I inquired, and Jay said, "That's not 4, that's 40!"

Concerned that I was getting to the correct answer too quickly, I pointed to the answer of 20 and asked, "Who got this answer?" Two children raised their hands and offered two different explanations. One said, "Four and 4 is 8, and 6 and 6 is 12; so 8 and 12 is 20." The other explained, "Four and 6 is 10, and 4 and 6 makes another 10; so 10 and 10 is 20." I responded that Jay had just said that the 4 didn't mean 4, but 40, and repeated the original problem, "How much is 46 and 46?" Several hands went up, and someone said, "Oh! It has to be 80 (meaning that 40 + 40 = 80)!" One went on to say, "Take 10 from 12 and add it to 80, and you get 90, and 2 left over is 92." At this point several children asked that their original answers be erased. This request proved that these children benefited from the higher-level arguments to which they were exposed.

THREE EXAMPLES OF MATH SESSIONS

Having discussed principles of teaching and children's inventions in general, I would now like to sketch how I proceed each day and how the discussions changed during the course of a year. To do this, I present three examples of sessions that took place one year in October, February, and May.

October 1

This was one of the days of filming to make the videotape *Double-Column Addition* (Kamii, 1989a). The problems I put on the board on this day, one at a time, were the following:

$$
\begin{array}{ccccc}
9 & 8 & 6 & 3 & 5 \\
+6 & +7 & 4 & 6 & 4 \\
& & +2 & +1 & 3 \\
& & & & +2 \\
\end{array}
$$

$$
\begin{array}{cccc}
13 & 17 & 26 & 4 \\
+13 & +13 & +5 & \times 5 \\
\end{array}
$$

We spent about 25 minutes discussing all the different ways the children invented.

February 5

This was another day of filming for the videotape. I put the following problems on the board, one at a time, and we spent about 30 minutes discussing all the different ways the children wanted to show off, before going on to a story problem:

```
    4        20        24        29        87
  + 4      + 50      + 53      + 35      + 24


  420      2680        18        17        26        24
+ 346    + 3319       -  6      -  9      - 17      - 14
```

The story problem I made up was: There are 65 second graders in this school when we put all three second-grade classes together. Twenty-six of the second graders ordered chicken for lunch, and the rest ordered soup. How many are getting soup? The answers the children gave were 39 (8 children), 41 (5 children), 34 (one child), and "Don't know" (9 children). When some children have no idea how to approach a problem, we discuss all the different ideas about how to set it up. I ended up writing the following on the board:

$$
\begin{array}{r}
65 \\
- 26 \\
\hline
\end{array}
$$

Joyce announced that she got as far as 60 − 20 but got stuck. Those who got the answer 39 explained it in one of the following ways:

$60 - 20 = 40$ $60 - 20 = 40$

$40 - 6 = 34$ $5 - 6 = 1$ in the hole, negative 1, or 1 below 0

$34 + 5 = 39$ $40 - 1 = 39$

The answer 41 to such a problem is well known to all second- and third-grade teachers. Some of our children get this answer by doing $60 - 20 = 40$, $6 - 5 = 1$, and $40 + 1 = 41$.

May 21

Most of the hour was spent on story problems, but I gave the following three computational problems first:

```
    28      1,568        87
  + 92    + 2,896      - 29
```

The first problem was easy for almost everybody, and about half of the children agreed that a good way to solve the second problem was the following:

$$1,000 + 2,000 = 3,000$$

$$500 + 800 = 1,300$$

$$3,000 + 1,000 = 4,000$$

$$4,000 + 300 = 4,300$$

$$60 + 90 = 150$$

$$4,300 + 100 = 4,400$$

$$4,400 + 50 = 4,450$$

$$8 + 6 = 14$$

$$4,450 + 10 = 4,460$$

$$4,460 + 4 = 4,464$$

The subtraction problem, $87 - 29$, demonstrated the usual difficulties. One-third of the class was fully confident about their answers as well as their reasoning, but the rest gave the usual kinds of answers: 91, 68, and 62. "Let's go on to something else," I said, because there is no point in making children do what is obviously too hard for them. (I later found out that this kind of problem is hard even for many fourth and fifth graders.)

The next problem I gave was the following story problem: There are three flies. If each fly has 46 suction cups on each one of its legs, how many suction cups are there all together? I immediately heard busy comments about whether the problem was 46×3 or 46×18. So I said, "Some people say the problem is 46 times 3, and some people say it is 46 times 18. Which one is it?" Someone answered, "Forty-six times 18 is right because each fly has 6 legs, and 6 and 6 and 6 is 18." There were lots of comments, and someone suggested, "Let's just go our own ways."

I went around the room to find out how the children were thinking, by looking at what they were writing. I then listed the following answers vertically on the board as the children announced them: 134, 138, 1,068, 876, 728, 148, and 828. Some children exclaimed, "Disagree!" when they heard the smaller numbers. As a result, the children who got the first two answers felt the need to check them and later asked me to cross them out.

"Who can prove that their answer is right?" I asked. I chose three children to come to the board, one at a time. They had all used addition in a variety of ways.

Chuck said, "Forty, 40, 40, 40, and 40, that's 200," and I wrote the following:

```
        40
        40
        40
        40
        40
       200
```

He went on to say, "Another five is 200, plus 200, and that's 400. We got rid of 10 of the 18. Five more is 600, and three more is 600 plus 120, and that's 720." Following his statements, I went on writing as follows:

```
        40
        40
        40
        40
        40
       200
       200
       400
       200
       600
       120
       720
```

Chuck then said, "Six 4 times is 12 and 12, and that's 24. Another 4 sixes is 48. That takes care of 8 of the 18 sixes. We need 10 more, and that's 48 and 12, which is 60. And put 60 with 48, and that's 108." Looking at the 720 I had written on the board, he then added 108 to it and announced that the answer was 828.

The second way of solving the problem was invented by Ellen and Cathy, who usually worked together. They started out by asking me to write "18 forty-sixes." (I encourage children to ask me to write on the board because they write so slowly that they lose the class' attention.) A summary of their procedure can be seen in Figure 6.1. Unlike Chuck, they used a great deal of writing. When they were finished and saw that their answer was the same as Chuck's, they jumped up and down with joy.

The third way of solving the same problem was invented by George. He began by asking me to write 40 six times in a column, six more times, and six more times, always in a column. After getting a total of 720, as

Figure 6.1. Ellen and Cathy's way of doing 46 × 18.

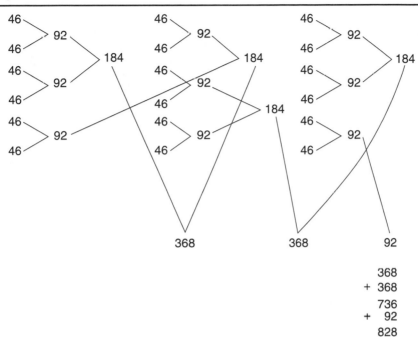

can be seen in Figure 6.2, he asked me to write three columns of 6 sixes. The rest of his procedure can be seen in Figure 6.2.

I went on to an easier problem: Let's suppose we have a beehive. In this beehive, there are 10 bees going to collect nectar. Each bee visits 36 flowers. How many trips did all the bees make all together?

Somebody immediately yelled, "That's 10 times 36!" Four different ways of solving this problem were volunteered. Carol got 30 × 10 = 300 by counting by tens. She then added the sixes as shown in Figure 6.3 and announced the answer of 360.

Jerry's way was similar, but he used a lot of writing and started out by asking me to write 10 thirty-sixes. Figure 6.4 illustrates his procedure.

I asked, "Does anyone have a way that is the fastest?" George offered the following argument:

$$10 \times 10 = 100; \text{ so } 30 \times 10 = 300$$

$$6 \times 10 = 60$$

$$300 + 60 = 360$$

Figure 6.2. George's way of doing 46 × 18.

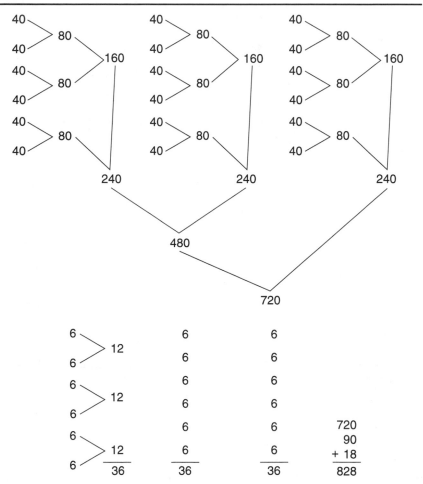

Cathy challenged him by saying, "Anything times 10 is the number with a zero. Always, all you have to do is add a zero to it. So 10 times 36 equals 360. That's all there's to it!" Surprised by this bit of knowledge (or trick), I said, "I want you to prove to me that 10 times 36 is 360."

Cathy came to the board with Ellen, and the two wrote the number 10 thirty-six times all over the board. They first counted the top row, "Ten, 20, 30, 40, 50, 60, 70," and wrote "70" for it. They then repeated this procedure twice but got confused and decided to start all over, from 10 to 360.

Figure 6.3. Part of Carol's work in computing 10 × 36.

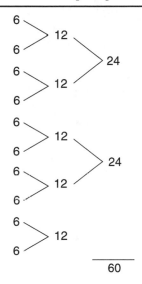

Figure 6.4. Jerry's way of doing 10 × 36.

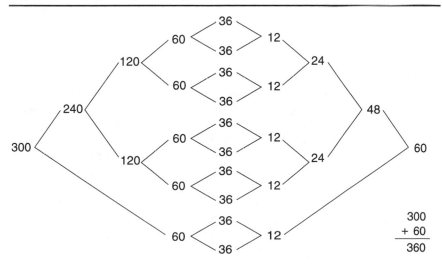

Before concluding this section, I would like to mention two ways of dealing with individual differences that work well. One is to write five or six problems on the board and ask each volunteer to choose the one he or she would like to solve. Below is an example of the choices a teacher may offer:

$$
\begin{array}{ccccc}
26 & 18 & 29 & 123 & 53 \\
+\,12 & +\,6 & +\,15 & +\,382 & +\,37 \\
\end{array}
$$

We have found that most children choose problems at the right level for them. They know which problems are too hard for them and which ones are boring. In an atmosphere that fosters children's development of autonomy, they seem to make decisions that are educationally appropriate for themselves.

The second way of dealing with individual differences comes from *CGI Mathematics: Classroom Action Research, 1997–98* (Abbott et al., 1998, p. 99). Below is an example of the five choices of pairs of numbers a teacher presented in giving a word problem:

> Lindsey had _____ chocolate chip cookies. At lunch she ate _____ of those cookies. How many cookies does Lindsey have left?
>
> 13,5   23,15   53,35   93,45   133,85

When we understand that word problems require the logico-arithmetization of reality, we can make the logic of the word problem the same for everybody in the class, while making the arithmetic part easier or harder.

CONCLUSION

I would like to end this chapter with a few comments about what children write or do not write during these discussions. As stated earlier, children are free to think when they are not required to write anything. This is why I ask them to put everything away at the beginning of our discussions. As we get to large addends in the hundreds or repeated addition such as 10 x 36, however, I see children writing on paper or on their desks. When they need to use writing to remember *the results of their thinking*, I let them use paper and pencil. This kind of writing is very different from the kind used in following the rules of "carrying" and "borrowing."

The value of emphasizing children's thinking was confirmed in May one year when Connie told me that the third graders receiving traditional instruction were being taught rules of writing to solve problems such as

$$2\overline{)84} \quad \text{and} \quad 3\overline{)93}$$

I decided to find out how my second graders approached these problems, and asked, "How would you divide 84 by 2?" In no time, at least a third of the class had the answer, without writing anything. They explained, "Half of 80 is 40, and half of 4 is 2; so the answer is 42." For 93 divided by 3, they had the same kind of argument: "Ninety is 3 times 30, and 3 is 3 times 1; so the answer is 31." Children who have not been made to follow rules of writing do their own thinking and do not become dependent on adults or on paper and pencil.

CHAPTER 7

The Use of Situations in Daily Living and Other Activities

by Linda Joseph

A CONSTRUCTIVIST MATH PROGRAM cannot be limited to the math hour, for two reasons. First, arithmetic is what children construct out of their real-life experiences, and not something that is put into their heads from textbooks. Second, teachers cannot turn children's mental activity on only during the math hour. If we want mentally active children during the math hour, we have to encourage them to put things into relationships and to be alert and curious throughout the day.

A constructivist teacher is constantly on the lookout for situations that can be used to develop children's numerical thinking. Some of these situations appear in daily, weekly, or monthly routines, such as taking attendance and lunch counts. Others appear fortuitously, as when a child says, "I have an odd number of holes [eyelets] on each side of my shoe, but when I lace it, it comes out even!" A third kind of activity, such as cooking, is a real-life activity that naturally occurs in children's lives but has to be planned by the teacher to happen in the classroom. In this chapter, I will give examples of each of these three types of activities I used as a second-grade teacher.

DAILY, WEEKLY, AND MONTHLY ROUTINES

Taking Attendance, Ordering Lunches, and Counting Lunch Money

Each morning upon entering the classroom, the children in my class performed a simple procedure that simultaneously served to take attendance and to record their choices for lunch. The children each had an assigned number from 1 to about 26 (depending on the class size) that corresponded to the class register, which was in alphabetic order. These numbers were written on small cards that were hanging on individual hooks on a bulletin board near the entryway to the classroom. Another part of the bulletin board was divided into three sections with three labels: "Regular lunch," "Soup," and "Brought lunch." Under each of these labels were four rows of five pins. The children each took the tag with their assigned number and hung it on a pin under the appropriate label. As class began, I asked, "How many regular lunches are we ordering today? How many soups? How many brought lunches?" and the children gave me a tally for each item. The next question, "Is anyone absent?" was answered by a glance to see if any tags were still hanging in their original positions. The children added together the three numbers for lunches and any absences, to make sure the whole class was accounted for.

After recording the lunch money received from individual children each morning, I used to invite two or three to add the total amount collected. Regrettably, lunch money is now computerized, but I have kept this real-life situation in the second edition of this book because there are other similar opportunities teachers can use to ask children to count money. Real-life situations are much better than mere exercises because they motivate children to be accurate for reasons that are real (rather than merely to satisfy the teacher).

The children had figured out the desirability of separating the money into checks, dollar bills, and coins, and counted the amounts in their heads in a way that surprised me at the beginning. Going through the checks, they usually added only the dollar amounts first. They then added the bills and took care of all the dollars. The next step was to combine the coins and the cents on the checks in some way that resulted in making dollars. They then ended by counting the leftover coins.

The following is an example. The money collected consisted of four checks (for $3.40, $4.25, $3.40, and $4.25), 5 dollar bills, 4 quarters, 6 dimes, and 3 nickels. One child found $14 altogether on the checks, added to this the dollar bills and got $19, and added the 4 quarters and got $20. He then counted the dimes and nickels and found 75 cents, put it with 25 cents on one of the checks, and announced, "That's 21 dollars." He then added the cents on the other three checks, found the total to be $1.05, and declared that the whole thing came to $22.05. I used to think that paper and pencil were indispensable for this chore until I saw the ingenuity of these second graders!

If children got different totals, those disagreeing with one another got together and started all over until they came to an agreement. Some children were not willing to try counting money at the beginning of the year. Most, however, did become interested by the end of the year.

Recording Time for Trips to the Bathroom

To encourage children to tell time, I posted a sign-out sheet near the door for recording bathroom visits. My rule was that two boys and two girls could go at one time. Each child going to the bathroom was asked to record the time he or she left the room and the time of return.

The children often checked one another with comments such as "You can't put 11:30 because it's not even 11 o'clock yet." The other might say, "Oh, it's 10:30!" I used to wonder why children waited by the door with a sheet and pencil in hand, and eyes raised to the clock. When I saw that it was 8:59, I realized that he was waiting for one more click to be able to record 9:00.

Voting

When autonomy is the aim of education, the teacher asks children to make decisions as much as possible. Therefore, children try to offer convincing arguments and call for a vote for everything from choosing games to deciding whether to go outdoors or stay inside and play. At one time the class often voted to choose between their two favorite whole-class games— Around the World (described in Chapter 6) or Tic-Tac-15 (described in Chapter 8). This was so often a topic of debate that the class decided to play the two games on alternate Wednesdays.

In voting, the children found that there was no need to count the opposing votes when there were only two choices. As long as the first group was more or less than half the class, they could proclaim the winner.

Going to the Media Center

We had an open Media Center, which meant that children could go at any time to check out books or to do their prescriptions. (I prescribed a particular center or topic of research, or the use of computers.) However, the children knew my rule that only six could go at a given time to the Media Center. Therefore, they often deduced whether they could go by making a quick count of the number of children in the classroom, the number gone to the bathroom, and the number absent.

Changing the Calendar

When one month ended and it was time to take off the old dates and put the new ones on the large calendar (a grid that had only the days of the week at the top), the children liked to help. To take advantage of their interest, the changing of the calendar was made into a large-group activity. I asked the children on what day of the week the new month would begin. Some could figure out the day of the week the following month would begin, before all the numbers had been replaced. One child's procedure for doing this was to count down 4 weeks from the first of the new month, advance to the next day (because $4 \times 7 + 1 = 29$), and add either 1 or 2 days, depending on how many days were in the month.

Ensuring That Game Pieces Are Not Lost

The children were responsible for making sure all game pieces were accounted for. Before each game, the groups counted to see if all the pieces were there. At the end of the game, they again counted to be sure all the pieces were put back. Small pieces often fell to the floor and would be lost if there were no count. The children knew that they needed to alert the rest of the class immediately if parts could not be found. They said, for example, "There's only 48 cards here. That means four are missing," or "I can find only 97 pieces for The Hundred Board. We have to find three."

Dealing with Overdue Books and Fines

Once a month, a list came from the Media Center concerning overdue books and fines. This list was posted near the door as a reminder, and the children often read it while lining up to leave the classroom. Sometimes someone remarked, "Wow, Becky, you owe 75 cents and 45 cents. That's over a dollar. You need to return two more books, too." Others crowded around and began adding their overdue fines. A few returned to their desks to write their totals down to take home.

Paying for School Supplies

We were permitted to sell pencils, paper, and other school supplies in the classroom to save trips to the office. This gave the children a chance to work with real money. The buyer and seller had to agree on the cost of each purchase.

When children needed pencils or paper but did not have any money, they were permitted to charge. They signed their names on a sheet of paper, along with the date, the items bought, and the amount charged. Periodically, the children added up the totals of each person's charges. One such example was, "Peter, you owe 15 cents and 50 cents." Another child said, "That's 65 cents," and Peter retorted, "That's 15 cents and 50 cents!"

One morning, we had almost no supplies left, and I asked Becky to go to the office to replenish our stock of pencils by getting five of each kind available. When she returned, the class was curious as to how many and what kinds of pencils she had. I asked them to figure out the total number by telling them that she had five of each kind and asking Becky how many different kinds she had brought back. When she replied "four," the classmates began chattering among themselves saying, "That's 4 fives," or "That's 5 times 4." Several asked, "Do you have 20 pencils?" They then crowded around, separating the pencils into four groups of five pencils to prove their answer, some commenting, "I got it right."

Paying for Popsicles on Birthdays

As mentioned in Chapter 5, parents often bought popsicles (25 cents each) for the entire class to celebrate their child's birthday. With a blank check to be filled in, the children eagerly began to figure out how much money was needed. Some children touched each desk, walking around the room saying, "Twenty-five and 25 is 50; 25 and 25 is another 50; so that's a dollar," and continued in this manner. Others looked at the tags on the lunch board and counted "One, two, three, four, that's a dollar." Others wrote down "25" many times, one for each child, and then counted four numbers and placed a "1" beside each group, until all the 25s were counted. If there was a disagreement, they started again, counting carefully.

Adding Numbers of Soup Labels

The school used to participate in the Campbell Soup Company's program that gives equipment to schools that collect large numbers of soup labels, and the class that had the highest number at the end of the collection period was treated to an ice-skating party. An enormous chart on the lunchroom wall had the names of all the teachers on the left side and the months across the top, so that the number of soup labels collected by each class could be recorded at the end of each month.

At the end of September, the children were delighted to be able to compare all the totals. At the end of October, the totals posted held a nice surprise: Our class had the highest total for that month. After seeing that, some children began to add the two monthly totals for every class. This ranged from 11 for one kindergarten class to over 400 for our own second-grade class. When they began adding the numbers for third grade, they found that one class had over 600 labels. Each month thereafter, at least five children excused themselves from games to add soup label totals and to return with their findings. I still marvel at these children's ability to add big numbers in their heads and to write only the totals in the thousands. Of the many visits to the lunchroom chart, only one child ever chose to waste time, and the others decided to send him back to class.

FORTUITOUS SITUATIONS

In addition to using routine situations that came up in the life of a second-grade class, I also made math lessons by picking up on children's spontaneous remarks. These remarks are important because they spring from the depth of children's thinking. The child's observation about the eyelets on his tennis shoes is an example that had not occurred to me. If an idea intrigues one child, it is likely to intrigue others who are at the same developmental level.

The following two activities sprang from spontaneous remarks that had too much potential to ignore until the next math period.

Pizzas

We were treated to a pizza party by a local pizzeria for winning a contest. (Prizes are not good for children's development of autonomy, but we cannot object to every contest sponsored by parents to raise money for the school.) When the boxes containing the pizzas arrived, I decided to spice the event up with a little arithmetic. I informed the class that each of the four pizzas would serve half the class. Someone immediately said, "That means there are 12 slices in each one because we have 24 here today." I then asked, "How many slices are there in all four boxes?" One of the quietest children raised his hand and confidently said, "Four times 12 is 48 because 12 plus 12 is 24, and two 24s is 48."

Tennis Shoes

As mentioned earlier, one day, just before our math period, Jerry commented, "I have an odd number of holes [eyelets] on each side of my shoe, but when I lace it, it comes out even!" When I asked the class if they had odd or even numbers of eyelets on their shoes, many admitted to not knowing what odd and even meant. I asked Jerry if he could explain, and he gave the following lecture.

He wrote the numerals 1 through 10 in a column on the chalkboard and drew the appropriate number of circles beside each one (see Figure 7.1). He then drew a ring around each pair of circles and explained, "Every time

Figure 7.1. Jerry's drawing to explain the meaning of odd and even numbers.

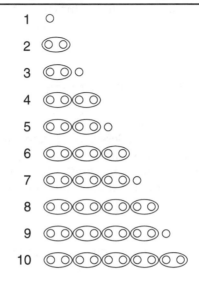

you see a circle without a partner, he's the odd man out. That makes the number odd."

When everybody knew what we were talking about, all the children wearing tennis shoes began counting their shoes' eyelets to determine whether they had odd or even numbers of holes. They had no need for further directions as they began milling about making their own analyses. They were delighted to find that not only did odd plus odd make an even number, but that two shoes or four odds were even as well.

Since not all children were wearing shoes with laces, they asked to repeat the activity the next day, when they would wear that kind of shoe. So on the following day, I asked each child to write on a card the number of holes in his or her shoes and then to choose a partner. The pairs of children mentally added the numbers written on their cards and checked their answers by physically counting the holes. Each couple then joined another couple and added the number of holes in all four pairs. They found that no matter how many pairs of evens and odds were added, they always ended with an even number.

TEACHER-PLANNED ACTIVITIES

The preceding two categories of activities were about situations that did not originate during the math hour. The third category consists of activities planned for the math period. While I generally spent half of the math period on the kind of discussions described in Chapter 6 and the other half on games, I sometimes introduced other types of activities, such as cooking and making parachutes. The reason for this must be obvious. Variety stimulates mental activity and pushes the frontiers of our thinking.

I begin with two cooking activities, go on to an estimation activity using M&M's, and end with the physics of parachutes.

S'mores

My student teacher introduced the activity of making S'mores, which are graham-cracker sandwiches baked in an oven until the filling, consisting of chocolate and six marshmallows, melts. She told the class that *they* had to figure out all the amounts that would be needed. She formed three groups and asked one to decide how many boxes of crackers were needed, another to figure out how many chocolate bars had to be bought, and a third to calculate whether one bag of miniature marshmallows was enough for everyone.

The student teacher handed a bag of miniature marshmallows to the marshmallow group and instructed them to find out how many were in the bag and whether that was enough for everyone to have six each. However, she asked them to estimate the number first, and some of their answers were 250, 150, 450, 199, 200, 660, and 312. Eric quickly figured out that 144 marshmallows were needed because "24 people times 3 marshmallows is 72, and if there are 6 per person, that's twice as many, and 72 plus 72 is 144." The children then began counting and found 636 in the bag.

Meanwhile, the student teacher told the chocolate-bar group that each bar had enough for four people. The children added 4 several times (4, 8, 12, and so on) and when they reached 24, they declared that they needed six bars of chocolate.

The graham-cracker group was a disaster. They had too many factors to contend with: Did one cracker make one S'more or two, since each cracker was to be broken in half? The fact that there were three packages in a box further confused them. The children physically broke each cracker into two pieces to see the top and the bottom and to count them as one S'more. They had to break and count all three packages, rather than use one package and triple it.

The following day the student teacher announced, "This is what you told me to buy yesterday. We'll throw out this box of crackers and open a new one. Let's count a package." (I would have preferred postponing the activity until the children figured out all the necessary quantities themselves. Adults often solve problems for children, thereby depriving them of opportunities to *think*.) Led by the student teacher, the class found 11 crackers in a package. Another package was counted, and again 11 were found. Finally, someone announced, "Eleven and 11 is 22! One box is enough because 22 and 11 is 33."

After distributing the crackers, marshmallows, and chocolate, the children assembled their ingredients. One asked, "How will we know which is whose?" Amy solved that problem by drawing a 3 × 4 grid on the chalkboard to show the arrangement of the cookies on the baking sheet. After placing their cookies on the pan, the children reported to Amy, who recorded their identification numbers in the corresponding spots.

Some children volunteered to be clock watchers, and I asked, "What time is it?" and "What time will it be in 3 minutes?"

"They are growing!" one child remarked. This was a good opportunity to teach the word *expanding* and to ask if someone could think of something else that expanded while cooking.

Doughnuts

Another cooking activity seemed good for graphing. The student teacher began by telling the class that we were going to make doughnuts using cans of refrigerator biscuit dough. As usual, she asked the pupils how many cans would be needed if there were 10 biscuits in each can. She then asked each child to decide which one of four colors they preferred for their glaze: red, blue, green, or yellow. Their replies were written on the board. Blue was favored by 14, yellow was chosen by 5, green by 3, and red by 2.

The student teacher then asked the children to draw a picture or make a graph to show how much glaze we needed for each color. Some made vertical or horizontal bar-type graphs. I was surprised by the large variety of products, samples of which are shown in Figure 7.2. There were three main categories. More than half of the children made graphs of some kind, as shown in Figure 7.2(a), while 29% represented discrete quantities without equal units on a line, presented in Figure 7.2(b), and 14% represented continuous quantities, shown in Figure 7.2(c). We had done one graphing activity earlier in the year, and I could see that children had benefited from it only if they were already at a certain developmental level.

M&M's

I brought out a 1-pound bag of M&M's one day and poured the contents into a transparent bowl, asking for estimations of the number the bag

Figure 7.2. Three categories of response to the teacher's request for a picture or graph to represent the class' color preferences.

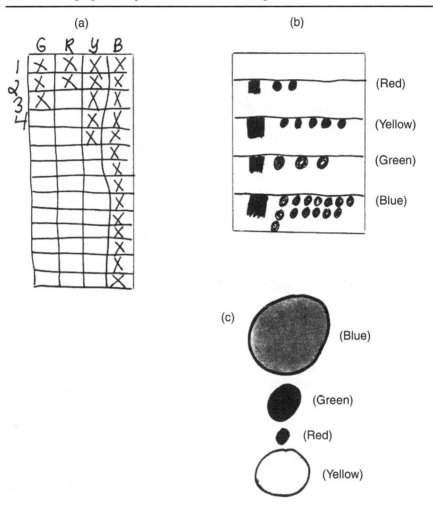

had held. This would have worked better by secret ballot because the children were influenced by one another's comments of "too high" or "too low." Most guessed fewer than 100, with the average about 50. The child with the highest guess, 200, was told that that many would have burst the bag.

When I asked for a quick and easy way to count the candy, one child said, "By tens," and another said, "By fives." They voted and decided to count by tens. When we reached 100 with nearly a full bowl left to go, they couldn't believe there could be another hundred. When we reached 200, they couldn't imagine having another hundred left. When we reached 400, with a dwindling number left in the bowl, they erroneously started saying that there were probably at least 600 or 700.

As each group of 10 tens was counted, the children put a circle of yarn around it, at my suggestion. Glancing into the bowl, which was nearly empty, I silently took over, arranging the remaining candy into two lines of 10, with 6 loose ones in another. I then asked each child to come up and count the entire amount silently and to write his or her answer on paper. Most did this effortlessly, and then compared answers. They finally agreed on a total of 426. One interesting note was the fact that, even though yarn was encircling each group of 100, most children counted as though the yarn were not there. The children counting by tens reminded me of Sharon Ross's (1986) study with lima beans (see Chapter 2). Some of her second graders counted the beans by ones after they had put 10 into each cup. My second graders counted the M&M's by tens, even though there was yarn around each group of 100.

I then asked, "If each person wanted to eat 10 candies, how many would we have to have, and would there be enough?" The solution took many forms, from counting people by tens to repeatedly writing down the number 10.

I then asked whether we had enough for us to have 20 each. This was much more difficult to figure, and we ran out of time, with only one child giving the answer: "If we need 250 for us to get 10 each, we'd have to add another 250 for us to get another 10 each, and that's 500; so we don't have enough." Several could see her reasoning and nodded in agreement.

The M&M's were handy for math problems in subsequent lessons. For example, I asked, "If there are 60 left, how many would these two children get?" The class was able to tell me quickly, "Thirty, because 30 and 30 is 60." When I asked them to split the M&M's among three people, they also could mentally make three groups, telling me to count by twos, changing the twos to twenties. Next, I asked them to divide the 60 candies among four, and in a few moments they again had figured it out mentally. When I asked how they knew, one said he just took five candies from each of the other three groups and gave those 15 to the fourth person, and that left the first three people with 15, too. Impressed by their thinking, I asked, "Do you think five people can share the candies equally?" The children again had the answer in just a few moments, without using paper and pencil. Half the class could solve this problem, but I have never seen a problem of this type in second-grade textbooks.

Parachutes

I conclude with an activity that combines physics and mathematics, or measurement, to be more exact. As stated in *Physical Knowledge in Preschool Education* (Kamii & DeVries, 1978/1993), young children think hard when they act on objects to produce a desired effect, can see the objects' reactions, and can vary their actions.

Our objectives for the day were to study children's methods of measurement, to observe how they worked, and to review terms such as *circle*, *square*, and *rectangle*. I displayed plastic garbage bags, string, yardsticks, and rulers, and told the children that they were going to design their own parachutes. Most of them decided to make rectangular or square ones. They paired themselves and began working eagerly. (Whenever possible, I asked children to work in pairs, to maximize both social interaction and independent work.) The yardstick or ruler was used occasionally, but only to make straight lines. As for the string, the children simply unwound a desired length and used it as a standard for the other pieces. In other words, no child used a yardstick or ruler to measure anything.

When all in the class had finished making their parachutes, I took them in small groups to the gymnasium, where we had a balcony on the second floor, to test how well their products worked. At their countdown, they let go and watched their creations drift to the floor. When I asked, "Whose won?" they indicated that the winner was the last one to touch the floor. Each subsequent group had a similar response.

After these empirical tests, I asked what it was that made a good parachute. The pupils looked blank for a moment until one said, "Sam made a good one." When questioned why his was good, they said, "Because it was slow coming down." When asked why his went slowly, Sherry replied, "I don't know, but his also went straighter." Sam said, "That's because Cary said to put a hole in the middle." Nearly everyone then cut a hole in the middle of theirs and began taking turns climbing on a stool to see if a hole helped control the descent.

At the end of the hour, I told the class, "You've had a day to experiment. Tomorrow, you and your partner are going to make two more parachutes. Make them alike in some ways and different in some ways. Try to figure out what makes a parachute better." The class had caught on quickly, and the next day most parachutes were designed like Sam's, with a hole in the top.

These three kinds of activities, some routine, some accidental, and some planned, all have a place in the classroom. The children show their fondness for mathematics when they exclaim, "We could do math all day!"

CHAPTER 8

Group Games

with Linda Joseph

GAMES CAN BE USED in ways that foster or hinder the development of autonomy. Since autonomy is the overall aim of education for us, we have given a good deal of thought to the ways commercially available and teacher-created games can be used to develop children's ability to think numerically as well as sociomorally. This chapter describes some of the games we have used successfully with second graders. Other games can be found in Wakefield (1998), and two excellent games (Knock-Out and Fudge) are listed in the Appendix. Principles of teaching, including how to introduce games, are described in *Young Children Reinvent Arithmetic* (Kamii, 2000, Chapter 13).

Games are difficult to classify because many (such as Four-in-a-Row, discussed later) can be used for addition or subtraction, and they can be made easy or hard depending on the numbers used. We nevertheless have organized them into three main categories: games involving addition, those involving addition and subtraction, and gamelike activities for the whole class. We hope readers will consider each game for possible modification.

Three points need to be mentioned about the following descriptions of specific games: First, when the number of players is not specified, it can vary from two to four, but three is generally ideal to maximize opportunities for mental actions. Second, complete source information about the games identified as commercially made is given in the Appendix, as are names of some of the mail-order firms from which games may be purchased. However, the sources of some games are unknown because the games were found in classrooms, described at conferences, or photocopied from various sources and passed around. Third, we never specify how the first player is to be chosen, and not all the details of each game are spelled out. The reason for this omission is that, for the development of children's autonomy, it is good that they have to make their own rules and decisions. When we define goals in the context of autonomy as the broad aim, we use math games for children's sociomoral development as well as for their construction of logico-mathematical knowledge.

Two problems frequently emerge in games: (1) Many children make a column of scores to be totaled at the end of the game rather than calculating and recording their cumulative scores as the game progresses, and (2) some children pay attention only to what they are doing and not to what others are doing. These problems prevent children from getting the full benefit of games, and ways of dealing with them are discussed at the end of this chapter.

The use of regular playing cards is often recommended in this chapter, but Rook cards (Parker Brothers, 1972) and Flinch cards (Parker Brothers, 1988; Hasbro, 1998) sometimes work better. Rook cards are numeral cards 1–14 in four different colors (a total of 56 cards). The Flinch cards currently available (Hasbro, 1998) consist of nine sets of numeral cards 1–15 plus nine cards without any numerals (a total of 144 cards, including nine cards without any numerals).

GAMES INVOLVING ADDITION

Basic Games

We single out certain games for later presentation because they offer advantages that many teachers prefer to consider separately. Those are games using dice in various ways, games involving physical-knowledge activities, and games involving money. The games described in this section are organized generally in order of difficulty, from those requiring the making of 10 with two cards to those involving much larger sums. To avoid frequent use of "his or her" and similar paired constructions, we will use gender-specific pronouns alternately. "His" or "her" is thus not meant to convey any assumptions about the gender of the players.

Making 10 with two numbers

This category is especially important because knowing all the combinations of two numbers that make 10 is useful in adding two numbers that total more than 10. For example, 8 and 4 can be added easily when we can think $(8 + 2) + 2$. The first three of the following five games (Tens with Nine Cards, Find 10, and Draw 10) are easier than the other two because they can be played by trial and error. In the last two games (Tens Concentration and Go 10), the players have to know what numbers to look for or ask for.

TENS WITH NINE CARDS

Materials: Homemade numeral cards, six each of numbers 1 through 9 (54 cards); alternatively, playing cards, ace through 9 (ace = 1).
Play: The first 9 cards of the deck are arranged as shown in the example in Figure 8.1. The object of the game is to find all the pairs of cards that make 10, such as the 9 and the 1, the 3 and the 7, and the two 5s. After taking all the possible pairs, the first player fills up the empty spaces with cards from the deck, and the turn passes to the next player.

The person who collects the most pairs is the winner.

FIND 10

Materials: Homemade numeral cards, six each of numbers 1 through 9 (54 cards); alternatively, playing cards, ace through 9 (ace = 1).
Play: The object of the game is to find two cards that make 10 (8 + 2, for example). The person who collects more pairs than anybody else is the winner.

All the cards are dealt except the last one, which is placed in the middle of the table, face up. Each player keeps the cards dealt, in a face-down stack, without looking at them.

When his turn comes, each person turns over the top card of his stack. If this card can be used with the one on the table to make 10, the player can take it and keep the pair. If the card cannot be used, the player has to discard his card in the middle of the table, face up. For example, if he turns over a 6 and there is only a 3 on the table, the player has to discard the 6, and the turn passes to the next player.

Figure 8.1. The arrangement of cards in Tens with Nine Cards.

Draw 10

Number of players: Four.
Materials: Homemade numeral cards, six each of numbers 1 through 9 (54 cards); alternatively, playing cards, ace through 9 (ace = 1).
Play: This game is played like Old Maid. One card is drawn from the deck and is set aside throughout the game, so that there will be an odd card without a mate at the end of the game. All the other cards are dealt.

Each player goes through the cards received making all the possible pairs that make 10 (6 + 4, for example). All the pairs thus made are stacked in front of each player.

The players then take turns, each holding her cards like a fan and letting the person to her left draw one of them without looking at them. If the person drawing the card can use it to make 10 with one of the cards in her hand, she adds this pair to her stack. If she cannot use it, she has to keep it in her hand. She then holds all her cards like a fan so that the person to her left can draw one of them at random.

Play continues until one person is left holding the odd card and loses the game. The one who made the most pairs is the winner.

Tens Concentration

Materials: Playing cards or homemade numeral cards, four each of ace (or 1) through 9 (36 cards).
Play: Twenty-five cards are placed in the middle of the table, face down, in a 5 × 5 arrangement. The players take turns turning over two cards, trying to make a pair that totals 10 (7 + 3, for example). If a pair can be made, the player keeps it and continues to play as long as he is successful. If he is not successful, he returns the two cards to their original face-down position and replaces any cards he took with new ones from the deck.

With 25 face-down cards on the table, the turn passes to the next player to the left.

The person who collects the greatest number of pairs is the winner.

This game can be varied by increasing the number of cards placed on the table. A 6 × 6 arrangement may be more challenging.

Go 10

Number of players: Three or four (two-player game is too easy).
Materials: Playing cards or homemade numeral cards, four each of ace (or 1) through 9 (36 cards).

Play: The object of the game is to make 10 with two cards (9 + 1, for example). All the cards are dealt. The players then lay down in front of themselves, face up, all the pairs that make 10. They then begin to ask specific people for specific numbers in a way similar to Go Fish. For example, John may say to Carol, "Carol, do you have a 1?" If Carol has a 1, she has to give it to John. John then lays this 1 and a 9 in front of himself, face up.

A player can continue asking for a card as long as she gets one that she requested. If she does not get a card she asked for, the turn passes to the person who said, "I don't have any." (Alternatively, the players can take turns in a clockwise direction.)

The person who makes the greatest number of pairs is the winner.

Making 10 with four numbers

TAKE TEN

Materials: A commercially made board (see Photograph 8.1) or a board made at home. There are 66 round cards bearing the numerals 1 through 7, plus a Joker, in the following quantities:

> 1: 22 cards
> 2: 16 cards
> 3: 12 cards
> 4: 7 cards
> 5: 4 cards
> 6: 2 cards
> 7: 2 cards
> Joker: 1 card

Play: The object of the game is to make 10 with four cards in a row, horizontally, vertically, or diagonally. All the cards are placed face down in the box, and each player takes three cards. Each in turn places a card on any one of the circles on the board that is not occupied. He then replaces this card with one from the box, so that he will have three cards again.

When a player completes a row of four cards that make 10, he collects the four cards. The joker can be used for any value. (The child in Photograph 8.1 knew that his opponent was holding the joker and chose to prevent his opponent from completing a row.)

The player who collects the most cards is the winner.

Photograph 8.1. Take Ten.

Making sums up to 12 with two or more numbers

Shut the Box

Materials: Twelve cards numbered 1 through 12; two dice; paper and pencil for scorekeeping.

This game is commercially available now (see Appendix), but the numbers in the commercially available games go only up to 9. Other versions with numbers to 12 sometimes can be found. A game using cards and dice is described here for those who do not have access to the commercially made game. The commercially made game is not essential, but it is desirable because children enjoy manipulating the flaps much more than cards.

Play: The 12 cards are arranged in a line in sequence from 1 to 12, face up. Each player in turn rolls both dice and turns over as many cards as she wishes, to make the total of the dice. For example, if she rolls a 6 and a 2, she can turn over the 8; the 1 and the 7; the 2 and the 6; the 3 and the 5; the 1, the 2, and the 5; or the 1, the 3, and the 4.

She rolls the dice again and keeps playing until she cannot make a total with the remaining cards. She then totals the number of points left on the cards remaining face up and records it. The turn passes to the next player, who begins with all 12 cards as before.

The points left at the end of each turn are added to the player's previous total. When a player reaches 45 points, she is eliminated. The winner is the last person to reach 45 points.

Making sums up to 15 with two or more numbers

QUINCE

Materials: Playing cards from ace through 10 (ace = 1); 10 counters for each player.

Play: The object of the game is to get as close as possible to a total of 15 without going over it.

The dealer deals two cards to each player, including himself, one at a time, face down. Each player looks at his cards without letting the others see them. The player to the dealer's left begins play. If his cards add up to less than 15, he may ask the dealer for another card, hoping to get one that will bring his total closer to 15. In turn, the other players, too, may ask for another card if they want to. A player may keep asking for another card every time his turn comes, until he is satisfied with his total and says, "I stand pat," or until he goes over 15 and is out of the game.

For example, in a two-player game, one receives a 6 and an ace. He knows that 6 + 1 is too low to win; so he asks the dealer for another card. If he receives a 2, he has only 9 points.

The dealer has a 9 and a 3. He could stop here but decides to ask for a card. If he gets a 5, he goes over 15 and is out, and the other player automatically wins the round and gets a counter.

If there are more than two players, all the totals are compared when all the players have finished asking for cards.

The player who has the highest total without going over 15 is the winner of the round and gets a counter. In case of a tie, there is no winner for the round.

The winner of the game is the person who collects the most counters, or the first person to collect 10 of them.

TIC-TAC-15

Number of players: Two (or two teams).

Materials: Paper and pencil (or a chalkboard and chalk).

Play: This is an excellent team game for the whole class, and Linda's class regularly played with great excitement.

A Tic-Tac-Toe grid is drawn, and the children take turns writing numbers in the spaces. The object of the game is to make a total of 15 with three numbers in a vertical, horizontal, or diagonal line.

There are two ways to choose the numbers that can be used by each player (or team). One way is for one player to use the even numbers (2, 4, 6, 8, and 10) and for the other to use the odd numbers (1, 3, 5, 7, and 9). In this game each number can be used only once. Another way of assigning the numbers is by using 10 cards numbered 1 through 10. The players (or teams) take turns drawing a card.

As variations, the total can be changed to 16, 20, or any other number, and the children can experiment with the numbers that can be used.

Making 20 with two or more numbers

TWENTY-TWENTY

Materials: A deck of playing cards from ace through 10 (40 cards); 24 counters or small tiles.
Play: Each player takes six counters and is dealt five cards. The remaining cards are placed on the table in a face-down stack. The players take turns putting one card down at a time next to one that is already on the table (see Figure 8.2). After putting down a card, each player takes the top card of the stack so that she will have five cards again.

Figure 8.2. Twenty-Twenty.

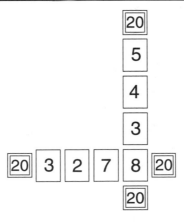

When a player puts down a card that makes a total of 20, either vertically or horizontally, she closes the line with two counters or tiles, as shown in Figure 8.2. The person who uses up her six counters first is the winner.

TENS AND TWENTIES

Materials: This is a commercially made game consisting of 48 sturdy, plastic triangles, with numbers such as those shown in Figure 8.3 (see Appendix). The triangles come in two sets. One set has red lines separating the numbers ranging from 0 to 10. The second set has green lines separating the numbers 0 to 20.

Play: The two sets may be used separately as two games or mixed together. The triangles are shuffled, face down, and divided equally among all the players. The first player puts down any triangle of his choice. In turn, each player then puts down a triangle in such a way that the numbers linked make a total of 10, if only the red set is used, or a total of 10 or 20, if both sets are used. Figure 8.3 shows an example of such a link.

The person who has used up all his triangles first is the winner. A player who does not have any triangle to play must pass.

A challenging version is to play alone so that each set of 24 triangles forms a hexagon with all the numbers correctly linked.

Figure 8.3. Tens and Twenties.

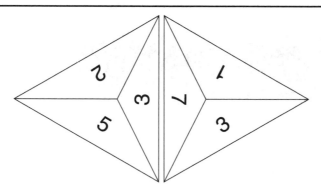

Making sums up to 21 with two or more numbers

BLACKJACK

Material: A deck of 52 cards with the following values: 2 through 10 are worth the values shown, the face cards are each worth 10, and aces are worth 1 or 11. Ten counters or blocks.

Play: This game is played just like Quince, except that the players try not to go over 21. The winner is the person who collects the most counters.

Making sums up to 30

BUTTERFLY

Materials: Forty playing cards, ace through 10 (ace = 1).

Play: Each player is dealt three cards, which remain face up in front of her throughout the game. Seven other cards are turned face up and shown in a line in the middle of the table. The rest of the cards make up the drawing pile.

   When her turn comes, each player picks up as many cards as necessary from the middle to make the same total as that of her three cards. When she cannot make any more sets of the same total, the cards that she took are replaced with cards from the drawing pile, so that there will be seven cards for the next player.

   The person who has the most sets at the end is the winner.

FOUR-IN-A-ROW

Number of players: Two.

Materials: A board such as the one shown in Figure 8.4; 26 transparent chips, 12 each of two colors, plus 2 of any color.

Play: Each player takes 12 chips of one color. Each in turn chooses two numbers on the small square, places the two chips of any color on these numbers, finds the sum on the large square, and covers it with one of his 12 chips. The object of the game is to be first to make a row of four with one's chips, vertically, horizontally, or diagonally. If a sum is already covered, the player wastes a turn. (Credit goes to P. Cobb, T. Wood, E. Yackel, G. Merkel, B. Gerald, M. Preston, and G. Wheatley for inventing these games and their variations.)

Variations: This game can be made much harder by using larger addends in the small square and changing the game to Five-in-a-Row, which ac-

Figure 8.4. Four-in-a-Row.

5	6	7
8	9	10
11	12	13

16	19	22	14	17
24	11	15	20	21
15	23	18	12	19
25	20	21	17	22
13	14	23	16	18

tually belongs to the next category (see Figure 8.5). Each player gets 18 chips in Five-in-a-Row. Below are two examples.

With addends of 37, 15, 17, 29, 19, 8, 45, 27, and 26 in the small square, the large square consists of 48, 66, 36, 60, 64, 43, 34, 72, 46, 34, 56, 82, 63, 37, 45, 44, 71, 42, 35, 42, 27, 74, 62, 23, 45, 32, 44, 53, 46, 42, 54, 25, 52, 56, 41, and 55.

With addends of 55, 22, 28, 42, 11, 37, 33, 19, and 45 in the small square, the large square consists of 83, 50, 64, 79, 77, 61, 92, 74, 33, 41, 52, 30, 70, 75, 88, 97, 59, 53, 48, 44, 61, 78, 87, 39, 47, 66, 64, 56, 65, 82, 70, 56, 67, 55, 73, and 100.

THIRTY MAX

Materials: The following 54 cards and paper and pencil for scorekeeping.

> 1–9: 3 cards of each number (27 cards)
> 10–19: 2 cards of each number (20 cards)
> 20: 6 cards
> Joker: 1 card

Play: Four cards are dealt to each player, and the remaining cards make up the drawing pile, which remains face down. The object of the game is to win points by arranging four cards that total up to 30 (see Figure 8.6). In Figure 8.6, the total of the four cards around the "20" is 4 + 12 + 7 + 6 = 29.

Each player must first put down a 20 (as shown in Figure 8.6) before beginning to arrange four other cards around it. If a player does not have a 20, she can do one of two things: (1) Take a card from the drawing pile, hoping to get a 20, or (b) use two of her four cards to make exactly 20. If the second alternative is chosen, the player can take only one card from the drawing pile and will have only three cards in her hand throughout the rest of the game. If the first alternative is chosen but a 20 does not come up, one card has to be discarded so that the player will have four cards again. This player will have a choice between the same alternatives on her next turn.

Once a 20 (or two cards that make 20) has been put down, the player can put down one card at a time in one of the four possible positions. The player then takes a card from the drawing pile to have four cards again (or three cards if the player used two cards to make 20). If the total of four cards exceeds 30, the score for that set is zero. If the total is 29, as in Figure 8.6, the score for that set is 29. The Joker can stand for any number desired.

Figure 8.5. Five-in-a-Row.

15	19	12
23	17	32
51	11	14

34	27	38	32	47	66
26	29	31	42	36	51
70	30	33	35	29	44
63	23	26	40	55	74
34	37	49	68	28	31
83	43	46	62	65	25

Figure 8.6. The arrangement of cards in Thirty Max.

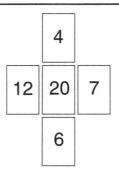

A player who has only big numbers in her hand that will make her total exceed 30 can start another set if she has a 20 (or two cards that make 20).

When a player has made a set of four cards, she records the total and discards the set onto the discard pile.

When there are no more cards left in the drawing pile, the cards in the discard pile are shuffled to have a new drawing pile. Before the game begins, the players have to agree on how many times the discard pile will be reshuffled. Alternatively, the rule can state that the first person to reach a cumulative total of 100 is the winner, or that the person who has the highest total is the winner.

Notes: (1) Children often add 20 and may need to be reminded that *only the four numbers around the 20* should be added. (2) This game appeals to more advanced second graders.

Making sums greater than 30

EVEN DOMINOES

Material: Dominoes; paper and pencil for scorekeeping.
Play: This is a game invented by children in Linda's class. The object of the game is to make points by making even-numbered sums. All the dominoes are turned face down. The players draw five dominoes each. One domino from the pile is placed on the table. The players take turns placing a domino so that the two touching ends (not the outer ends) make an even number. For example, if a 6–3 domino is on the table, the next player can play either a 0, 2, 4, or 6 on the 6 end; or a 1, 3, or 5 on the 3 end, since those combinations make even numbers. After each turn, the players draw another domino so that they always have five. A player's score is the total made with the two touching ends.

The players keep cumulative scores, and the first one to reach 70 wins. In another version, the players continue to play until all the dominoes are played; and the highest score wins.

Materials: A deck of 52 cards with the following values: Ace is worth 1; 2 through 10 are worth the values shown; and the face cards are each worth 10 points.

Play: Each player is dealt four cards, and the remaining cards make up the drawing pile. The players take turns taking the top card of the drawing pile and discarding one of the five cards that are in their hands. The object of the game is to make the largest total value possible (or the smallest).

When a player thinks he has the largest (or smallest) total, he says, "Knock-knock," and everybody else has one more turn. The person having the greatest (or smallest) total is the winner.

Materials: The following 44 cards (no longer commercially available but possible to make); paper and pencil for scorekeeping. To make the cards, buy a large sheet of cardboard at an art supply store and cut it into 44 pieces (6 cm × 2 cm). Also needed are a package of self-adhesive circles in assorted colors (preferably red, yellow, blue, and green, ¾ inch in diameter, like Dennison No. 43-851); Scotch tape to put on both sides of the cards after affixing the circles, to protect them from wear.

Three colored circles are placed on each card. Eight of the cards should have three circles of the same color: two all-green (G), two all-yellow (Y), two all-red (R), and two all-blue (B) cards. The other 36 cards should have circles of two or three different colors, as follows:

BBG	BBY	BBR	GGB	GGY	GGR	YYG	YYB	YYR
RRB	RRG	RRY	GBG	GYG	GRG	BGB	BYB	BRB
YGY	YBY	YRY	RGR	RBR	RYR	GBY	GYB	GBR
GRB	GYR	GRY	BGR	BGY	BYR	BRY	YGR	YBR

Play: The object of the game is to win the greatest number of points by making lines of three or more circles of the same color, vertically, horizontally, or diagonally.

All the cards are mixed, face down. Each player takes three cards. To begin the game, one card from the face-down pile is turned over and placed in the middle of the table. When her turn comes, each person plays a card trying to make the maximum possible number of points. If she cannot make any points (i.e., if she cannot make an alignment of at least three circles of the same color with her card), she has to play a card anyway. After playing a card, she replaces it with one from the face-down pile.

The players put down one card after another, next to one that is already on the table, until a row of 11 is made. As shown in Figure 8.7(a), the cards can be placed either to the right or to the left of the card already placed, but they cannot stick out below or above the alignment.

When one row of 11 cards is completed, the next player can start at A, B, C, or D in Figure 8.7(b), and the others proceed in the directions indicated by the arrows. However, once a row is begun, it has to be completed before a new one can be made. (For example, once a player has put down a card at A, the next player can put one down either at B or next to A, but not at C or D.) Four rows are made by the end of the game (4 × 11 = 44).

Figure 8.7. The arrangement of cards in Dominique.

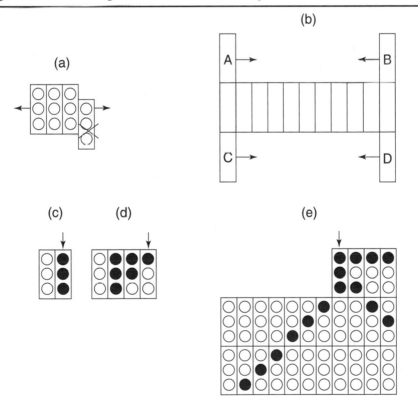

Points: A player wins points by putting a card down in such a way that her card makes a line of three or more circles of the same color, vertically, horizontally, or diagonally. If the circles make a vertical or horizontal line, the player gets 1 point for each circle. If the line is diagonal, she gets 2 points for each circle. Each player announces the number of points she got. If she fails to notice points she could have claimed, she is not entitled to them after announcing her total; the person who notices the oversight gets these points. The following are three examples of play and scorekeeping.

In the move in Figure 8.7(c), the player gets 3 points because she made a vertical line by playing a card that had three circles all of the same color.

Figure 8.7(d) shows a move for which the player gets 9 points (3 for the horizontal line and 6 for the diagonal line).

In the move in Figure 8.7(e), the player gets 29 points (4 for the horizontal line, 3 for the vertical line, and 2×4 and 2×7, respectively, for the diagonal lines).

We ask children to write their cumulative total at the end of each turn, as shown below. (If they erase the previous total, their arithmetic cannot be checked later by the teacher or anyone else. If they record only the number of points earned on each turn, they cannot know who is winning from moment to moment and will have to add a discouraging number of points at the end of the game.)

Brent	Liz
3	3
+ 3	+ 3
6	6
+ 6	+ 4
12	10
+ 3	+ 6
15	16
+ 6	+ 9
21	

TRI-OMINOS

Materials: A commercially made game consisting of 56 plastic triangles with a number from 0 to 5 on each corner of the triangle (see Appendix); paper and pencil for scorekeeping.

Play: All the Tri-Ominos are turned face down and mixed, and each player takes nine if there are two players, or seven if there are three or four players.

   One Tri-Omino is placed face up in the middle of the table to begin the game. The players then take turns putting down a Tri-Omino that has a side bearing the same two numbers as a Tri-Omino that is already on the table, such as in the move shown in Figure 8.8.

   Points are made by adding the three values shown on the face of the Tri-Omino that has been played. If the first player begins the game by playing the Tri-Omino on the right-hand side, he gets 25 points (5 + 5 + 5, plus a bonus of 10 points for starting the game). The second player gets 11 points (5 + 5 + 1). The winner is the person who has the greatest number of points at the end or the first person to reach a certain number of points. Other details of the game—in particular, other bonuses that can be earned—can be found in the instructions that come with the game.

Games involving repeated addition

I Doubt It

Number of players: Three or four.
Materials: A deck of 40 homemade cards, four each of 10 numbers such as the following:

   2, 4, 6, 8, 10, 12, 14, 16, 18, and 20
   5, 10, 15, 20, 25, 30, 35, 40, 45, and 50
   1, 3, 5, 7, 9, 11, 13, 15, 17, and 19

Play: All 40 cards are dealt. If the numbers on the cards are multiples of 2, the first player puts a 2 in the middle of the table, face down, saying "Two." The next player then puts a 4 on top of the 2, also face down, saying "Four." The third player continues with a 6, saying "Six." Anyone who

Figure 8.8. The placement of a Tri-Omino.

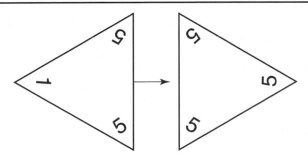

does not have a card she needs uses another card hoping to get away with this bluff.

Anyone who thinks that a card other than the one announced has been played says, "I doubt it." If the doubt is verified, the person caught must take all the cards on the table and add them to her hand. If the doubt is not verified, the accuser has to take all the cards. Play continues until a person wins by getting rid of all her cards.

As a variation, this game can be played using the numbers in descending order (20, 18, 16, etc.).

CHOOSE

Materials: Six ¾" cubes, each with different numbers and colors on its sides; paper and pencil for scorekeeping. Self-adhesive labels in assorted colors (such as Dennison No. 43-851) can be placed on the cubes, and numbers can be written on them with the combinations listed below. (Scotch tape protects the cubes from wear.)

	Green	Red	Blue	Yellow	Orange	Orange
First cube	1	5	2	6	3	4
Second cube	2	1	6	5	3	4
Third cube	3	6	4	1	2	5
Fourth cube	4	2	5	3	1	6
Fifth cube	5	4	3	2	1	6
Sixth cube	6	3	1	4	2	5

The six colors (column headings) indicate the six colors of stickers on the sides of each cube. The numbers are those that must be written on the stickers. For example, on the first cube, 1 should be written on the green sticker, 2 on the blue sticker, 3 and 4 on orange stickers, 5 on the red, and 6 on the yellow.

Play: The object of the game is to get the greatest number of points with cubes of the same color or the same number. In each turn, a player can roll the dice three times.

After the first roll, the player decides whether he will choose the same color or the same number. He sets aside those he wants to use and rolls the other cubes again. He can roll all six cubes again if the outcome of the first roll was not favorable.

After the second roll, the player sets aside the cubes he wants to use and rolls the others. He also may change his objective, depending on what he has gotten so far. If nothing encouraging has come up so far, he may roll all six cubes again.

After the third roll, the points obtained are written on the scoring sheet and added to the previous total. If, for example, the player gets 3 fours, his score is 12. If, on the other hand, he gets 3 green circles with a 6, a 5, and a 3 on them, his score is 14.

When all six cubes show the same color or the same number, this is called "Double Choose," and the number of points is doubled. For example, if the player gets 6 sixes, his score is 72 [$6 \times 6 \times 2$ or $2(6 + 6 + 6 + 6 + 6 + 6)$].

Board Games Using Dice in Various Ways

Board games using dice are singled out as a separate category because many kinds of dice can be used in a variety of ways for specific purposes. For example, Double Parcheesi (Kamii, 2000, pp. 174–175) uses a regular die, but players move twice as many spaces as the number rolled. If a player rolls a 9, for instance, she moves 18 spaces. Ten- and 12-sided dice permit the increase of addends to 10 or 12. Dice also can be used in other ways, such as the following:

1. *Set partitioning of 10.* Players subtract the number rolled from 10 to determine how many spaces they may advance. Thus, if a player rolls a 1, she can advance 9 spaces; if she rolls a 2, she can advance 8 spaces, and so forth.
2. *Set partitioning of 7.* Players can advance by the number that is on the bottom of the die, but no one can look on the bottom. If a player rolls a 6, for example, he can move 1 space after *mentally* subtracting 6 from 7.
3. *Moving only if the total is an even number.* A player can advance only if the total of the two dice is even; if it is odd, the person cannot move.
4. *Repeated addition.* If some spaces on a board say "×2" or "×3," the player doubles or triples the number rolled while on that space.
5. *Subtraction.* The smaller of the two numbers rolled must be subtracted from the larger.
6. *Addition and subtraction.* The numbers on two dice of the same color must be added, and the number on the die of a different color must be subtracted. If the result is smaller than zero, the player must move backward.
7. *Using doubles and doubles + 1.* Doubles are spontaneously used by many children, who change 3 + 4 to (3 + 3) + 1, for example. Teachers can experiment with putting different numerals on two six-sided dice. To encourage the use of doubles, try putting only two numbers on each

die (e.g., two dice, each with 3 threes and 3 fours on it). Following are several possibilities of combinations that can come up.

Numbers on each die	Possible combinations
3 and 4	3 + 3, 3 + 4, and 4 + 4
4 and 5	4 + 4, 4 + 5, and 5 + 5
5 and 6	5 + 5, 5 + 6, and 6 + 6
6 and 7	6 + 6, 6 + 7, and 7 + 7
7 and 8	7 + 7, 7 + 8, and 8 + 8

In another variation, only three numbers are put on each of two dice (e.g., each die having 2 sevens, 2 eights, and 2 nines on it). There are then the following possible combinations:

Numbers on each die	Possible combinations
7, 8, and 9	7 + 7, 7 + 8, 7 + 9, 8 + 8, 8 + 9, 9 + 9

Paths on boards can vary in shape, length, and content, and some commercially made games use only one marker, while others use two, three, or four. By "content" we mean the theme used in a game, such as dinosaurs, space shuttles, and football. We have found that a theme can contribute greatly to the popularity of a game. Parcheesi involves a path that goes around the board. Other shapes are a winding path, an 8-shaped path, a spiral path, a circular path, and a zigzag path. Hideout, described next, uses a circular path in an unusual way.

HIDEOUT

Materials: A board such as the one shown in Figure 8.9 and Photograph 8.2.; two dice; a marker for each player.
Play: Each player puts her marker on one of the starting spaces. Players take turns rolling the dice and moving as many spaces clockwise as indicated. (Refer to the preceding discussion about changing the rule for using the die or dice.) When a player lands on a space with an arrow, she follows the arrow into the space indicated. On her next turn, she moves clockwise as many spaces as indicated by the dice.

If a player's move brings her to a space already occupied, she must move her marker to where it was before. If a player lands on a green space, she gets an extra turn. If she lands on a red space, she will miss her next turn. The winner is the first to reach the hideout in the center.

Figure 8.9. A Hideout board.

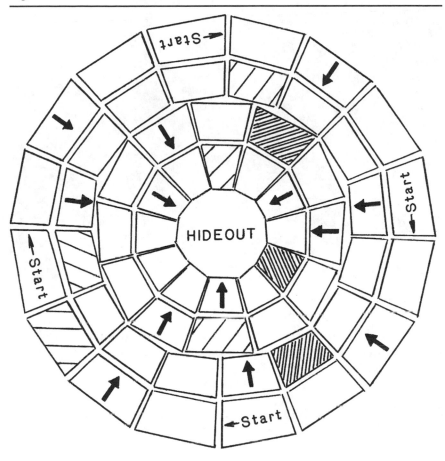

Start →

Start →

← Start

HIDEOUT

← Start

DOUBLES COVER-UP

For low-performing children, the teacher can make a board such as Doubles Cover-Up (see Figure 8.10). This game uses a die and as many transparent chips as there are numbers to cover. Two players sit on opposite sides of the board. If a player rolls 1, he covers the 2 on his side of the board; if he rolls 2, he covers 4, and so forth. If a number is already covered, the player cannot cover anything. The person who covers all six numbers first is the winner.

The preceding game can be modified into Doubles + 1 Cover-Up. In this case, a 10-sided die can be used with 20 transparent chips, and the board

Photograph 8.2. Hideout.

would include ten numbers from 3 to 21 (3, 5, 7 . . . 21). If a player rolls a 1, he covers 3 (1 + 1 + 1); if he rolls a 2, he covers 5 (2 + 2 + 1), and so forth.

COVER 20

Materials: A board with the numbers 1 through 20 for each player (see Figure 8.11); four 8-sided dice; 20 transparent chips for each player.

Figure 8.10. A Doubles Cover-Up board.

2	4	6	8	10	12
DOUBLES COVER-UP					
2	4	6	8	10	12

Play: Before each turn, each player decides whether to roll one, two, three, or all four dice. After rolling the die or dice, she covers the number or numbers corresponding to the total rolled. For example, if a 4, a 5, and two 3s are rolled, the player can cover 15, 10 + 2 + 3, 1 + 2 + 3 + 4 + 5, or any other combination that totals 15. The person who covers up all 20 numbers first is the winner.

Games Involving Physical-Knowledge Activities

Examples of games involving physical-knowledge activities (Kamii & DeVries, 1978/1993) are those that require aiming, such as basketball, pool, and golf. These games all involve an object's reaction to the child's actions of throwing, hitting, kicking, and so forth. They are treated as a separate category because some of them can be used outdoors, and the addends can be anything ranging from 0 to 3,000.

An advantage of this category of games is that some children learn much better when they can move around. For example, Linda Joseph taped a 3 × 3 grid on a desk, put a number in each section of the grid, and let children take turns throwing three cotton balls (or beanbags) onto the desk. A player's score on each turn was the total of the numbers indicated by

Figure 8.11. A board for Cover 20.

1	2	3	4	5
6	7	8	9	10
11	12	13	14	15
16	17	18	19	20

the three cotton balls. The players calculated a cumulative score at the end of each turn. For some children, the freedom to move around made an enormous difference in their enjoyment and learning of addition.

The following are some examples of physical-knowledge activities, grouped according to children's actions, such as throwing and hitting. Some are homemade games, while others are commercially made. Many commercially made games can be adapted and made inexpensively at home.

Throwing

Toss Game

Materials: A floor or desktop target; three poker chips. The target can be made from spongy foam packing material with holes cut in it. Numbers are written beside each hole, with the bull's-eye having the highest value and the numbers getting smaller away from the center.
Play: This is a variation on the game just described using a grid and cotton balls or beanbags. Each turn consists of tossing three poker chips onto the target.

Basketball

Materials: Old tire and rope; balls or beanbags. Old tires can be suspended and used for a "basket."
Play: Children throw a ball through the tire, getting 2 (or more) points per basket.

Ring Toss

Materials: A wooden board with hooks and numbers on it, as shown in Photograph 8.3; five rubber rings; paper and pencil for scorekeeping. This game is no longer available, but a version with sticks on a stand can be found in catalogs (see Appendix).
Play: The game in Photograph 8.3 came with 13 rings, but we used only five of them. After throwing the five rings, the children added the total to their previous score. The children decided where to stand to aim, and when the game ended.

Safe Dart Game

Materials: Dartboard and three safety darts, as shown in Photograph 8.4; paper and pencil for scorekeeping. Similar games are available through catalogs (see Appendix).

Photograph 8.3. Ring Toss.

Photograph 8.4. Safety Darts.

Play: The numbers of points each part of the board earns often need to be changed. Those on the board in Photograph 8.4 are 100, 75, 50, and 25. The players decide where they must stand to aim, and how many turns each person will have.

Hitting or pushing with a stick

GOLF, HOCKEY, AND POOL

Materials and play: These are all similar games that can be set up with an enclosure made with blocks. A stick, a chopstick, or a long block can be used to hit or push a ball or disk. The target can be a ball, an area taped on the floor, or an opening between two blocks. Children can decide on the number of points each successful attempt will earn.

Other physical actions

THE SPINNER GAME

Materials: A commercially made wooden bowl (called Roulette in some catalogs) with numbered holes and a spinner (see Photograph 8.5); six wooden balls.
Play: The printed instructions are good and can be used, but we prefer to modify the rules as follows to encourage children to make multiples of 10.

The six balls are placed in the middle of the bowl, and the spinner is spun so that it will knock the balls into the numbered holes. Points can be earned only in multiples of 10. For example, if the balls land in the holes numbered 12, 4, 2, 16, 3, and 9, one player may find only 20 points (16 + 4), while another may find 30 points (16 + 12 + 2). A third player may find 40 points (16 + 12 + 9 + 3). The player who gets the greatest number of points is the winner.

While the numbers on the commercially made game work adequately, the educational value of the game can be improved by taping numbers such as the following over them: 2, 3, 4, 5, 6, 7, 8, 9, 11, 12, 13, and 24.

SHOOT THE MOON

Materials: This is a commercially made game (see Appendix).
Play: The child has to make a steel ball go up an incline by increasing the distance between two steel rods (see Photograph 8.6). A player tries to get the ball as far up the incline as possible before it drops between the rods.

Photograph 8.5. The Spinner Game.

Photograph 8.6. Shoot the Moon.

The farther the ball goes before it drops into one of the holes below, the more points the player gets. The point system for Shoot the Moon and two possible modifications can be seen in the following list:

Shoot the Moon	*Modification 1*	*Modification 2*
−250	−10	−11
250	10	11
500	20	22
1,000	30	33
2,000	50	55
3,000	100	100

LEVERS

Materials: Base-ten blocks make a good lever, as can be seen in Figure 8.12. *Play:* Children can set up small boxes and make up a point system.

DOMINOES

One day, Linda Joseph came with a wooden ball about 2 inches in diameter and asked the class if they could think of a game that used it. One child immediately suggested rolling the ball to knock dominoes down. A player's score would be the number of points on all the dominoes knocked down, the child said.

Games Involving Money

Games involving money are singled out as a separate category because money is especially important in real life and its units entail dealing with addends of 1, 5, 10, 25, 50, and 100.

Figure 8.12. A lever made with base-ten blocks.

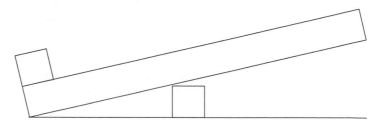

The Allowance Game

Materials: Commercially made game, which comes with a board, play money (20 five-dollar bills, 25 one-dollar bills, 20 quarters, 20 dimes, and 20 nickels), a die, four markers, and eight chips. (The one listed in the Appendix is best for second graders.)

Play: The children move a marker the number of spaces indicated by the die. They then follow the directions on the space they land on to know how much they earned or are to spend. For example, one space says, "Deliver papers. Earn 85¢," and another says, "Buy school stuff. Spend $1.00." The first person to have a total of $10.00 is the winner.

Coin Dice

Materials: Three coin dice (see Appendix) showing a penny, a nickel, a dime, a quarter, and a half-dollar. Also, 68 homemade cards such as the following (two of each unless indicated otherwise in parentheses; the cents sometimes should be written with a cents sign and sometimes with a decimal point):

3¢	35¢	75¢ (1)
7¢	36¢	76¢ (3)
11¢	40¢	80¢
12¢	45¢	85¢
15¢ (1)	51¢	$1.00
16¢	52¢(3)	$1.01
20¢	55¢	$1.05
21¢	56¢ (3)	$1.10
25¢	60¢	$1.25
27¢	61¢ (3)	$1.50 (1)
30¢ (1)	65¢	
31¢	70¢	

Play: Each player takes 16 cards and makes a 4 × 4 arrangement as in a Bingo game (see Figure 8.13). The players take turns rolling the three dice. Everybody who has a card corresponding to the total of the three dice turns it over. The person who first turns over four cards in a row vertically, horizontally, or diagonally is the winner.

As a variation, the first person who turns over two rows of four cards can be the winner. Another variation for winning is turning over the four corners first.

Figure 8.13. The arrangement of 16 cards in Coin Dice.

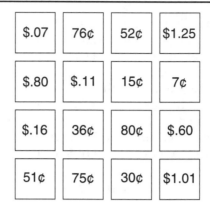

GAMES INVOLVING ADDITION AND SUBTRACTION

Card Games and Games Resembling Card Games

SALUTE!

Number of players: 3.

Materials: A deck of playing cards, with the face cards removed; ace = 1. (When children are beginning to play this game, it is good to use cards up to 6 and gradually increase the numbers to 7, 8, and so on.)

Play: The cards are dealt to two of the three players. The two players sit facing each other, and each holds his stack face down without looking at the cards. Simultaneously, the two then take the top cards of their respective piles and say "Salute!" as each holds a card on his forehead so that he can see the opponent's card but not his own.

The third player (who can see both cards) announces the total. Each of the other two players tries to figure out the number on his card, by subtracting the opponent's number from the total. The person who shouts the correct number first takes both cards. The winner is the person who collects more cards.

As a variation, this game also can be played with multiplication and division.

ADDITION AND SUBTRACTION SHAPES

Materials: Two sets of 24 commercially made sturdy plastic triangles like those made for Tens and Twenties (see Appendix for catalogs that sometimes list them). One set has red lines and involves addition. The other has yellow lines and involves subtraction with numbers up to 20. The two sets can be combined but also can be used separately.

Play: All the triangles are placed face down on the table, and the players each take an equal number, such as four. One triangle is turned over in the middle of the table to start the game. The players take turns matching a problem (such as 13 – 4) with an answer (such as 9).

Each time a player puts down a triangle, she replaces it with one from the face-down pile. A player unable to make a match must continue to take triangles until she gets one that she can play.

The winner is the first person to use up all her pieces.

CLOSEST TO 10

Materials: A deck of Rook cards (four each of 1–14; see Appendix), which can be homemade; paper and pencil for scorekeeping.

Play: Each player is dealt three cards. The object of the game is to use addition or subtraction with two of the three cards dealt to make a number as close to 10 as possible. There can be five or more sets, and the person with the lowest total score is the winner. Figure 8.14 is an example of a score sheet showing that Sarah won after five sets by getting a total of 7 points. (It is not always necessary to record the cards received, but we can see from this score sheet that Sarah's first set consisted of a 1, a 1, and a 14, and she did 14 – 1 = 13. Since the difference between 13 and 10 is 3, her score for the first set was 3.)

Each player keeps the card not used and is dealt two new cards for the next set.

ALWAYS 12

Materials: Seventy-two cards (which may be round, as shown in Figure 8.15) bearing the numbers 0 through 6 in the following quantities:

0: 8 cards
1: 10 cards
2: 12 cards
3: 14 cards
4: 12 cards
5: 8 cards
6: 8 cards

Also needed is a board with a cross showing four sections (or a sheet of paper creased to show four sections) so that cards can be stacked in each section.

Figure 8.14. Closest to 10 score sheet.

	Sarah			Jeff		
Set	Cards received	Computation	Score	Cards received	Computation	Score
1	1 1 14	$14 - 1 = 13$	3	12 10 2	$12 - 2 = 10$	0
2	1 2 14	$14 - 2 = 12$	2	2 8 3	$8 + 2 = 10$	0
3	1 4 10	$10 - 1 = 9$	1	14 10 3	$14 - 3 = 11$	1
4	4 8 3	$8 + 3 = 11$	1	10 12 7	$12 - 7 = 5$	5
5	4 6 7	$4 + 6 = 10$	0	10 8 9	$10 - 8 = 2$	8
Total			7			14

Play: The object of the game is to make a total of 12 with four cards. All the cards are scattered, face down, and each player takes three cards. When his turn comes, each player puts a card on a quadrant and then takes one from the box to have three cards again. Empty quadrants must be filled before cards can be placed on top of another. (See Figure 8.15 for several examples of this process.) The person who makes a total of 12 with four cards can take the four cards, as shown in Figure 8.15(a).

Figure 8.15(b) already has a total of 12. If the next player puts a 0 in the empty space, he can take the four cards, as shown in Figure 8.15(c). If he has only 5s, he is forced to make a total of 17, as in Figure 8.15(d). If the next person puts a 1 on the 6, as in Figure 8.15(e), he makes a total of 12 and can take the four cards. The 6 underneath his 1 is left for the next set, as well as any other cards that may be underneath the other three cards.

The person who gets the most cards is the winner.

Figure 8.15. Always 12.

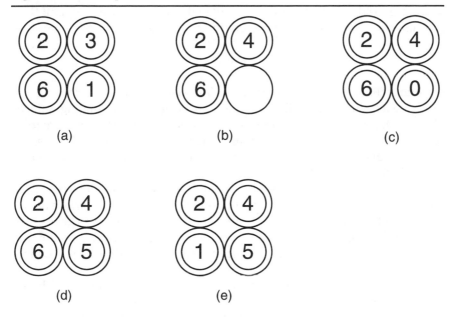

(a)   (b)   (c)

(d)   (e)

24 GAME, ADD/SUBTRACT PRIMER

Materials: A box of 24 Game, Add/Subtract Primer, which can be found in many catalogs (see Appendix). Use only the 2- and 3-dot cards, which are at appropriate levels of difficulty.

Play: Each card has two wheels and a target number (such as 24), and on each wheel are three numbers (such as 12, 14, and 2). The object of the game is to choose the wheel that has the numbers with which the target number can be made using addition and/or subtraction. All the players look at the same card trying to be first to make the target number. All three of the numbers on a wheel must be used *once* (and only once).

The first person to make the target number can take the card if she can explain how she made it (for example, $14 + 12 = 26$, $26 - 2 = 24$). The winner of the game is the person who collects the most cards. If an error is noticed, the player who is first to point it out gets the card.

A disadvantage of the version published recently is that the correct solution is printed on the reverse side of each card. We recommend cutting off the correct solutions before introducing the game to children. The reason is that children are *not* motivated to *think hard and debate* if they can find the correct solutions by looking at the back of a card.

LINEUP

Materials: Fifty-eight tiles bearing the following numbers: 1 through 10 (five of each, totaling 50 tiles); –5 and –10 (four of each, totaling 8 tiles). *Play:* Each player takes a –5 and a –10 tile first. All the other tiles are then scattered on the table, face down, and each player takes five of them, for a total of seven. One tile is then turned over and placed in the middle of the table to begin the line.

The players take turns adding a tile to the original tile, forming a line, and the object of the game is to be the one who gets to 45 points exactly. For example, if the first tile is a 7 and the players in turn put down a 10, a 3, a 10, and an 8, the next player can win the round if she puts down a 7. After putting a tile down, each player replaces it with one of the face-down tiles, to have seven tiles again.

A player who goes over 45 points loses the game and is out. The –5 and –10 tiles can be played at any time, but players learn to keep them to use them advantageously when they are in danger of going over 45 points.

Tally marks or objects can be used to keep track of the number of rounds won. However, our children simply go on to the next round without further ado.

THE ZERO GAME

Materials: A deck of playing cards; 10 counters for each player or paper and pencil for scorekeeping.
Play: All the odd-numbered hearts are eliminated from the deck. The face cards can either be eliminated or count as 10s. Each player is dealt three cards, and the players take turns putting a card down, face up, and subtracting the number on it from the previous total. The game starts with 30, and if the first player puts down a 10, he says, "Twenty" as he puts it down. If the next player puts down a 5, he says, "Fifteen." The person who goes below 0 is the loser of the round and receives a tally mark or a counter. The game is over when someone gets 10 tally marks.

The hearts (even-numbered) are "plus" cards, so the numbers on them are added to the previous total.

Each time a player puts down a card, he replaces it with one from the drawing pile to have three cards again.

Two to Four Cards

Materials: A deck of playing cards (ace = 1, face cards = 10).
Play: Four cards are dealt to each player. The top card of the remaining stack is turned over and shows the target number, which stays in the middle of the table. Each player tries to make the target with two to four cards, using addition and/or subtraction. For example, if the target number is 6, and the cards received are 2, 4, 8, and 8, a player can do 2 + 4 and get two cards, 8 − 4 + 2 and get three cards, or 2 + 4 + 8 − 8 and get four cards. The person who has collected the most cards at the end is the winner.

When a player cannot make the target number, she passes and returns her four cards to a discard pile. When a player finishes her turn, the unused cards also are returned to the discard pile. The target-number card, too, is returned to the discard pile at the end of the round.

Four more cards are dealt to each player for the next round, with a new target number. When there are no more cards remaining in the deck, the cards in the discard pile are shuffled and used again.

Anyone who catches an error made by somebody else gets a card from the person who made the error.

Excuse Me!

Materials: The following 42 cards; 60 counters, which are each worth $100; paper and pencil for scorekeeping.

    1 through 10 of spades are "minus" cards.
    1 through 10 of all the other suits are "plus" cards.
    Two Jacks

Play: The object of the game is to have more money than anybody else at the end. Five cards are dealt to each player. The remaining cards are placed in the center of the table, face down, as the draw pile. The top card is turned over and placed next to the draw pile to start the discard pile. If it is a Jack, it is put back in the draw pile and the next card is turned over. The counters are placed in a pile near the center of the table, and each person gets $200. Each player's money *must be kept in view* throughout the game.

The players take turns putting a card on the discard pile, face up, and taking one from the draw pile (to have five cards again). Each player adds to or subtracts from the running total and announces the new total. In the example in Figure 8.16, the running total is 0.

Figure 8.16. A cumulative score of 0 in Excuse Me!

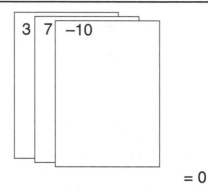

= 0

A player whose card brings the discard pile to exactly 0, 25, 50, 75, or 100 wins $200 from the center pile. A player who brings the discard pile to exactly 33, 66, or 99 can take up to $200 from one of the other players, saying "Excuse me!"

A Jack can be played on any turn and lets a player take $200 from one of the other players.

The discard pile can start with a negative number. But if it is confusing to start with a negative number, the rule may be changed to: The first number has to be 1 or larger. If the discard pile totals 100, a "minus" card or a Jack can still be played. Once the discard pile goes over 100, a new discard pile must be started.

When there are no more cards in the *draw pile,* a new one can be made by shuffling the cards from an old discard pile.

No one can go into debt. If someone has only $100, another player can take only $100 from him.

It is helpful to write the numbers 0, 25, 50, 75, and 100; and 33, 66, and 99 to keep in view, along with where $200 can come from when someone makes these numbers. It is also helpful to write down the cumulative totals.

Another version with 61 homemade cards: The following 61 cards are used:

−1 through −10	One card each
1, 2, 3, and 5	Three cards each
4, 6, 7, 8, 9, and 10	Five cards each
Excuse me!	Four cards
Very sorry!	One card
Revenge!	Four cards

The game is played in the same way as the 42-card version except that the "Very sorry!" card lets a player take $400 from any player, and a "Revenge!" card can be played only by a player who has just lost money because of an "Excuse me!" or a "Very sorry!" card. A "Revenge!" card entitles a player to take back the amount of money lost, plus $100.

Board Games

The Hundred Board

Materials: The unnumbered side of a Hundred Number Board (a 10 × 10 grid); a set of Hundred Number Tiles bearing the numerals 1 through 100 (see Appendix).

Play: This game encourages children to think about the spatial arrangement of 10 more, 10 less, 10 more + 1, 10 more − 1, 10 less + 1, and 10 less − 1. All the tiles are scattered, face down. Each player then takes eight tiles and keeps them face up in front of herself.

One tile is then turned up and placed in the appropriate space on the board. (It is surprising how hard it is for many second graders to decide where 68 should go, for example.) The players then take turns placing one tile at a time on the board and replacing it with one from the face-down pile. Only tiles that touch either a side or a corner of a tile already on the board can be played. For example, if 68 has been placed on the board, the tiles that can be played next are 57, 58, 59, 67, 69, 77, 78, and 79, as shown in Figure 8.17. (This may seem easy, but a surprising number of second graders do not notice that they can play the 57, for example.)

If a player does not have a tile that can be played, she has to miss a turn and take one from those that are face down. The first person to use up all her tiles is the winner.

A variation is to start the game with 1 in the space where 5 usually goes.

One Hundred Fifty, Exactly

Number of players: Two.

Materials: The numbered side of a Hundred Number Board (with numbers 1 through 100 in a 10 × 10 arrangement, see Appendix); three dice; a marker for each player.

Play: This is a game invented by children in Linda's class. The players take turns rolling the three dice, adding the results, and moving their markers. If the first player gets a total of 16, for example, he places his marker on

Figure 8.17. The placement of numbers on the Hundred Number Board.

57	58	59
67	68	69
77	78	79

16. If he gets a total of 12 on his next turn, he mentally adds this number to his previous total and moves his marker to 28, and so forth.

The object of the game is to reach 100 and then start at the top at 1 again and go to 50 (which makes 150). If a player cannot land exactly on 50, he subtracts his roll and goes backward. He continues to go back and forth on subsequent turns until he lands exactly on 50.

THREE-IN-A-ROW

Number of players: Two.
Materials: A board such as the one shown in Figure 8.18; two small paper clips; 16 transparent chips, eight each of two colors.
Play: This game is similar to Four-in-a-Row (described earlier). Each player takes all the chips of one color. Each in turn chooses one number from square A and one from square B and puts a paper clip on each number. She then subtracts the smaller from the larger, finds the answer in the large square, and covers it with a chip. If the number is already covered, this turn is wasted. The first player to get three chips in a row—vertically, horizontally, or diagonally—is the winner.

ZIGZAG

Materials: The Zigzag board shown in Figure 8.19; three dice; a marker for each player.
Play: All the markers are placed on "Start." The object of the game is to to be first to reach "Goal."

Figure 8.18. Three-in-a-Row.

14	13
12	11

9	7
5	3

A   B

6	10	7	9
2	4	5	3
7	5	6	8
4	9	8	11

Figure 8.19. A Zigzag board.

Goal								
2	9	7	4	6	8	7	5	9
5	4	3	8	9	1	2	5	4
8	7	6	3	5	4	9	2	7
6	2	5	7	8	7	6	4	3
8	7	3	6	4	1	2	5	1
2	4	8	5	9	7	6	8	5
7	3	2	1	5	4	5	7	3
5	8	7	2	8	7	6	9	8
8	4	5	6	7	3	6	5	3
2	8	1	8	10	7	9	4	5
7	5	6	9	4	2	8	1	3
Start								

The players take turns rolling the three dice. The three numbers rolled can be added or subtracted in any order of one's choice. For example, if a 2, a 3, and a 4 come up, they can make 9, 1, 3, or 5 in the following ways:

9: $(2 + 3 + 4)$
1: $(2 + 3 - 4)$ or $(3 + 2 - 4)$
3: $(2 + 4 - 3)$ or $(4 + 2 - 3)$ or $(4 - 3 + 2)$ or $(2 - 3 + 4)$
5: $(4 - 2 + 3)$ or $(4 + 3 - 2)$ or $(3 - 2 + 4)$ or $(3 + 4 - 2)$

The player thus can put her marker on 9, 1, 3, or 5. Thereafter, a player can move only one space at a time, forward, backward, sideways, or diagonally. For example, if a player is on 5 in the bottom row, he can move to 7, 2, 8, 1, or 6.

The first person to reach "Goal" is the winner.

TRIBULATIONS

Materials: 26 cards, two each of numbers 0 through 12; 49 ceramic square tiles (ceramic bathroom tiles are heavier and stay in place better than plastic tiles) bearing the numbers 1 through 8 in the following quantities:

1: 5 tiles
2: 6 tiles
3: 6 tiles
4: 6 tiles
5: 6 tiles
6: 10 tiles
7: 5 tiles
8: 5 tiles

Alternatively, gameboards similar to the one in Figure 8.20 can be made and photocopied, but many boards have to be made because children remember where to find combinations that make certain numbers (such as $5 + 5 - 5 = 5$).

Play: The tiles are mixed and randomly arranged into a 7 × 7 square as shown in Figure 8.20. The numbers can face in different directions.

The first player draws a card, announces the number, and places it where all the players can see it. Looking at all the tiles, all the players silently try to find three numbers in a row that will produce the number on the card. *The first two numbers must be added, and the third number must then*

Figure 8.20. Making 5 with 9 + 1 – 5 and making 10 with 6 + 5 – 1 in Tribulations.

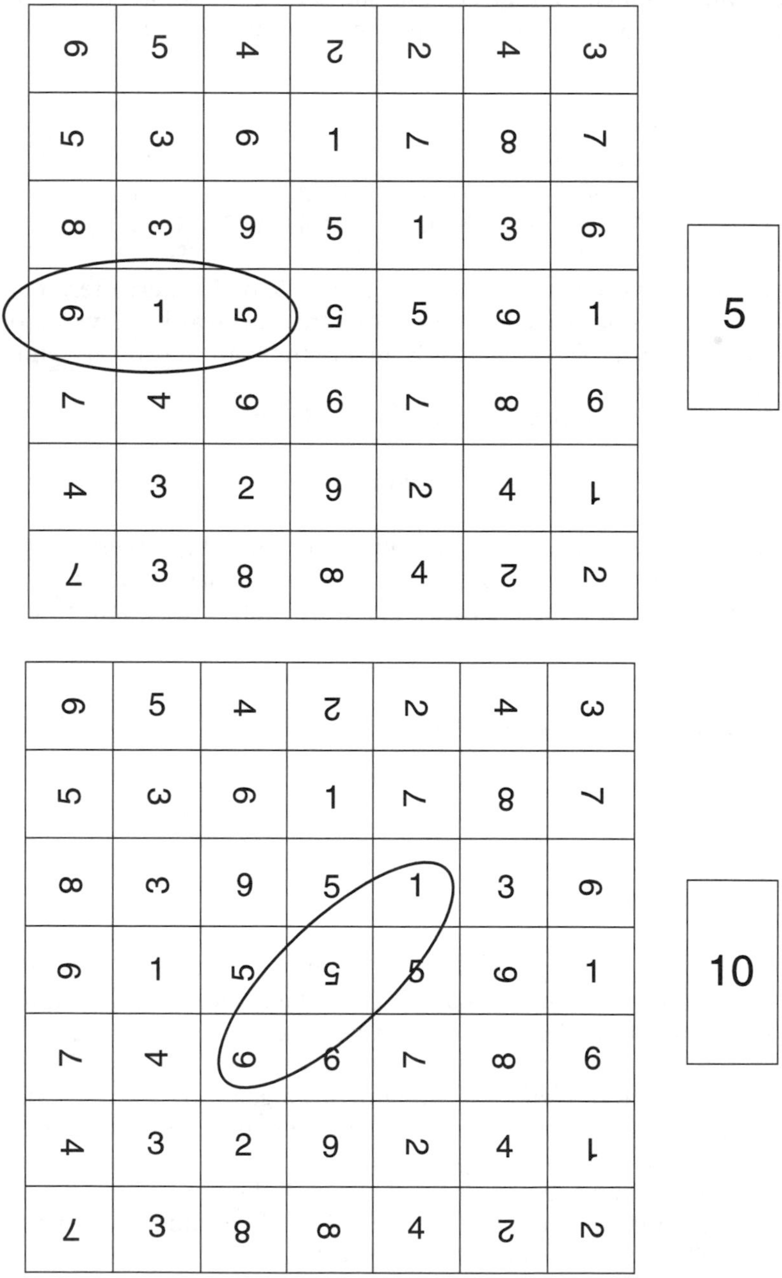

be subtracted to produce the number on the card. The three numbers must be in order vertically, horizontally, or diagonally in either direction. The 6s and 9s are interchangeable. In the first example, 5 was produced with 9 + 1 – 5. In the second example, 10 was produced with 6 + 5 – 1.

The first person to find a correct number combination announces it and collects the card if she can prove its correctness. A new card is then drawn, and play continues. The person who collects the most cards is the winner.

It is hard for many second graders to arrange 49 tiles, but the spatial thinking involved in making this arrangement is good for them. Some teachers prefer the photocopied version and have made multiple copies of each board so that each player can turn the board in various directions and touch the numbers being considered.

A WHOLE-CLASS GAMELIKE ACTIVITY

All the games described in this chapter so far are for small groups of two to four children. It is sometimes desirable to play games with the entire class to enhance a feeling of community in the room. Tic-Tac-15 was described earlier in this chapter as a team game that the class played often, with great excitement. Around the World, which was mentioned in Chapter 6, is also an exciting game children begged to play.

What's My Rule? is not exactly a game in which children try to win, but it is a whole-class, gamelike activity. Because it has a rule stating that no one can state the rule, it cleverly involves all class members, whatever their level of development.

For example, the teacher writes "3" on the chalkboard, draws an arrow from it, and then writes "7," as shown in Figure 8.21(a). She then writes another number and an arrow, as shown in the same figure.

The children who have an idea about the number that might go after the arrow raise their hands. If the child called on says "11," the teacher writes it and goes on to write another number and an arrow, as shown in Figure 8.21(b). The rule of this game is that the children can give numbers generated by following the rule they hypothesize, but they cannot state the rule itself.

The beauty of this game is that the less advanced children can have time to think, without having the rule stated by the more advanced students. In fact, the less advanced children can use the numbers given by the more advanced ones. By the time the column looks like Figure 8.21(c), all the children raise their hands.

Figure 8.21. An example of What's My Rule?

	(a)	3 → 7		(c)	3 → 7
		7 →			7 → 11
					18 → 22
					25 → 29
	(b)	3 → 7			36 → 40
		7 → 11			48 → 52
		18 →			59 →

The series ends when someone gives an incorrect number or says, "Disagree." The teacher then asks, "What's my rule?" and calls on someone to give it. She then starts a new series.

This game can, of course, be adapted for all the other operations.

CONCLUSION

We conclude with a few remarks about the importance of whole-class discussions and two problems we have encountered: One involves score-keeping, and the other concerns children who do not pay attention to what others are doing.

Whole-class discussions about specific games make an enormous difference to the value of each game. Immediately after the games are put away, the teacher may ask, for example, "Who had a problem that you'd like to discuss about Thirty Max?" One child may say, "We kept adding the 20 that was part of the bunch of cards," and the teacher may ask who else had this problem. If some students did not have this problem, the teacher may ask what they did differently. One student may explain, "I remembered to add only the four numbers *around* the 20, but not the 20." In this situation, the teacher may ask the student to arrange the cards in front of the class to demonstrate what he means.

Another student may bring up another problem: "I kept getting zero points by going over 30." The teacher may ask if anybody has any advice to offer, and an advanced student is likely to say that he plans in advance that if a maximum of 30 must be made with four cards, it is best to have about 7 on each card because $7 + 7 = 14$, and $14 + 14 = 28$. Somebody else may then add that if one card has a big number, like 13, he can compensate for it by looking for a small number, like 2. Advanced students like to talk about the strategic *thinking* they do, and less advanced students often benefit from what the advanced students say.

We often recommend scorekeeping on paper, but second graders tend to do two undesirable things: (1) They record a score after each turn but do not add it to the previous total, and (2) they erase the previous cumulative total and write only the new one. The first tendency is undesirable because players cannot tell who is winning from one moment to the next, and children do not learn arithmetic if they begin to add numbers only after the teacher announces that it is clean-up time.

Children's tendency to erase is undesirable because other people cannot check the computation if the numbers have been erased. Also, by examining children's score sheets afterwards, the teacher and parents can tell which game each child played, what numbers the student worked with, and what errors were overlooked. Furthermore, score sheets serve as records of children's progress over the year and enable the teacher to steer individual children toward certain games that are at their level.

The teacher can bring up these problems at class meetings, and explain why these are problems for him or her. Children respond well to these whole-class discussions because every member of the community can bring up a problem and ask for help in solving it.

An advantage of games over worksheets is that, in games, children can supervise each other and speak up immediately when an error has been made. We have observed, however, that some students seldom pay attention to what others are doing. This problem, too, can be brought up by the teacher, and students often suggest the introduction of a penalty. If a player can earn points by catching errors, the penalty motivates children to pay attention to what others are doing.

Autonomy is both moral and intellectual, and this aim guides the teacher in deciding how to interact with children before, during, and especially after the games. When we make decisions *with children*, we help them develop morally and intellectually from within. Children like to play math games and want to become competent players. Games can be used well or poorly, and the teacher's guidance makes an enormous difference to children's development of fluency in computation.

PART IV

A Teacher's Perspective and Evaluation

CHAPTER 9

Metamorphosis

by Linda Joseph

HAVING TAUGHT SECOND GRADE for 10 years, I thought I was a "good" teacher, who supplemented the basic mathematics textbook with manipulatives to illustrate my points and help my students understand the lessons. Therefore, when Connie Kamii came into my room, I thought she would be impressed with my class' performance and my teaching style. Instead, she said, "Your children are not thinking." It dawned on me that she was right, because I often had said to myself, "My students are not using their heads." Her idea was to use situations in daily living and games to encourage children to build their own knowledge of arithmetic.

I was somewhat afraid of launching into unfamiliar territory and of giving up my teacher's manual. However, I decided to see for myself if there could be a better way of teaching arithmetic. I began to change my strategy. I started planning ways of challenging the children instead of providing them with model solutions to imitate. I was skeptical, but, as my principal said, the old ways didn't work either. I had little to lose and much to prove to myself.

Most of the first year was a replication of *Young Children Reinvent Arithmetic* (Kamii, 1985), so I will briefly describe my observations of the first year and go on to the second, third, and fourth years.

THE FIRST YEAR

Throughout each school day, I encouraged the children to make decisions concerning numbers, whenever possible. For example, I encouraged them to divide birthday treats and to tell me what to write in the daily attendance report and lunch orders for the cafeteria. I even began to say, "We have spent 5 minutes so far. If we combine 5 minutes for everybody here, how many minutes have we spent all together?" Math thus was no longer something dished out on a piece of paper that was to be filled in with right or wrong answers. In fact, since we were not using worksheets or a textbook, paper was rarely used at all. Math became something that occurred whenever a question concerning numbers came up, and I stopped saying, "We aren't doing that today" or "Wait until math time," and began to say, "Let's find out now," as if that question were the most important part of our day.

I found that autonomy was necessary for games to succeed. If children came over asking me to settle arguments during game time, I told them that they could handle the arguments themselves. I knew the children were getting the idea when I overheard someone say one day, "She won't do anything right now. Let's go back and play." At the end of games, however, I sometimes asked, "Were there any problems today?" or "Did anyone do something that you would like to tell the class about?" This was the time when agitated children could ask for suggestions about their earlier complaints. The other pupils offered ideas about how to handle problems, such as voting to send a misbehaving child back to his or her seat. These discussions led to the children becoming more self-governing and left time for me to concentrate on the games. I had not counted on this bonus.

I found that, as my role changed from being the omniscient authority to one who asked for suggestions, I had to shift my focus away from myself as the central figure around whom classroom life revolved. This was not limited to math time. Instead of giving directions, I asked for children's ideas, such as where to put their artwork while it dried. This process, which Piaget calls "de-centering," challenged me to think about each situation from the child's point of view. It was the hardest thing for me to do.

Nobody had ever told me to make math fun. No one had ever said, "Math can be so exciting!" But that is what happened when I allowed, encouraged, and even enticed children to construct numerical ideas for themselves. I, too, invented my own procedures for encouraging children to construct.

I had begun the year with a lot of uncertainty; however, having seen how positively the children reacted, I could hardly wait to start the second year. I was curious to see whether the next class could attain the same heights.

THE SECOND YEAR

Starting the second year was easier, since I had survived one year without a textbook or workbook. In addition, the group of children coming to me for second grade had already spent first grade in a classroom where Connie's approach was used.

Since most of the children were familiar with games from first grade, I selected some that they already knew and put them out on a shelf. I then reviewed briefly a few games at a time and asked the children to choose a partner and a game. I gave guidance to those who needed it, and the first few days were devoted only to games.

While the children were playing games, I tested them individually on sums up to 9 + 9, to determine who knew their sums quickly and who counted on fingers (see Kamii, 2000, Tables 5.1 and 5.2). (I did this twice more during the year, while the children played games.) With this knowledge, I gently steered children toward games that would help in their weak areas. For example, to those weak in doubles, I suggested that they might like to play Double Parcheesi (Kamii, 2000, pp. 174–175).

I liked to know and remember who was playing which games, so I began to keep a small notebook in which I jotted down names, dates, and games, and any difficulties the students were encountering. The best way for me to tell a child's ability, though, was actually to play with him or her. By playing with the children, I could assess firsthand how well they reasoned with numbers.

When parents came for conferences, I could give specific facts, such as, "Your child knows the sums up to 10 quickly and easily, as well as the doubles up to 7 + 7. He has difficulty with sums between 11 and 18, so we have been playing Quince together." If a parent offered to help by drilling the child with flashcards, I quickly declined. I showed the article by Madell (1985) saying that memorization of "facts" is not desirable, and I asked them to help instead by playing games in which the child does most of the decision making.

Also in September, I began the discussions described in Chapter 6. This was an area lacking during the first year. These discussions were important for the exchange of ideas, and they proved to be most beneficial. My purpose was not just to get the class to agree on an answer; it was also to help children feel comfortable enough to present their ideas, even if they sometimes got stuck without getting the final answer. I also wanted them to see that there were many "right" ways to solve a problem. The discussions in September usually followed half an hour of playing games. By October, however, I had reversed the order and was beginning the math period with the discussions.

By early October, the children were accustomed to voicing their opinions by saying "Agree!" or "Disagree!" and had become adept at noticing at what point a classmate's thinking became flawed. It was not unusual, for example, to hear one pupil say to another, "I agree with the first part, but you forgot to add the other 10; so I disagree." The children had to choose their words carefully to make their ideas clear enough for the others to understand. If not, someone was bound to say, "That doesn't make sense to me." My role as teacher, then, was one of helping the children clarify their statements. They came to expect a variety of answers, since I often listed them on the board. Some children remarked, "Wait. I want to check mine," before explanations were begun, especially if there were many different answers. I was careful to create a climate in which the students felt comfortable when others had a different opinion.

Occasionally, I asked the children to write their answers on paper. This helped me know who wrote 10013 for 113, for example. When this happened, I asked the class how they thought the number should be written. Discussions of this type seemed to result in permanent learning much more often than did direct teaching.

By November, the range of ability had begun to widen tremendously. Having become adept at double-column addition, some children began requesting "something harder." The discussions then began to focus on whatever these challenge seekers wanted to do. If they said, "Give us something in the hundreds," a few children attempted those. By continuing to give a variety of easier problems, I could keep the others involved, too.

At that time of year, interest in games was lower because of children's excitement about becoming able to solve double-digit problems. The children often said, "Let's do brain exercises." That was our favorite term for problem solving at the board. I was thrilled with the children's excitement. They were stretching their ability and loving it. They especially enjoyed story problems involving multiplication, which they tackled in original ways. To do 12×6, for example, they made the following computations: $12 + 12 = 24$, $24 + 24 = 48$, $48 + 24 = 72$. No problem was too hard for them, as long as I gave them enough time to work it out. As a teacher, I was more like a scribe, writing on the board for the children while they concentrated on the thinking part, or asking just the right questions if they were floundering. When children figure out their own answers, ones that make sense to them, they are jubilant and gain confidence.

During a faculty meeting in January, a first-grade teacher asked Connie if we as teachers should be providing specific activities with subtraction. Her reply was that there was no point in "teaching" subtraction in first grade (see Chapter 5) and that children would be able to subtract when they were sufficiently adept at adding. Feeling that my children were adding quite well, I challenged them with the following problem:

$$\begin{array}{r} 46 \\ -18 \\ \hline \end{array}$$

One child best summed up the class' feelings by saying, "That's the hard kind." After a long pause, Eric said, "Forty take away 10 is 30, and 8 take away 6 is 2." Being familiar with this kind of error, I shook my head and told him that he could not subtract upside down. He ignored me and continued, "And 30 take away 2 is 28." I was dumbfounded to find that he got the correct answer, so I wrote a similar problem on the board. His method worked again and again. Eric explained that you could take only 6 from 6, but you still had to take 2 more from somewhere; so you took it from 30. My reaction was one of wonderment. It was such a simple solution. Other equally impressive methods followed on subsequent days.

I was becoming convinced by now that games and discussions were much better than drill sheets. The children reacted positively to my excitement and were willing to try any kind of problem. They even tackled division problems with ease. Their method of dividing 93 by 3 was, "You have 3 thirties in 90. Then, 1, 2, 3; so the answer is 31."

Throughout January and February, we varied math time to include only games on some days and only discussions on other days, but most days included both. This was a time when one child after another, almost daily, became able for the first time to attempt double-column addition and subtraction involving "regrouping," and they were succeeding in their attempts.

In March, the children were again eager to play games, especially Around the World, which was their favorite. Other frequently played games were Shut the Box, Dominique, Four-in-a-Row, and the Allowance Game (see Chapter 8). The children also enjoyed making up their own versions of dominoes and games using the Hundred Board. During discussion time, they looked forward to the story problems I made up, and frequently organized themselves into small groups to discuss the strategy that worked most quickly.

This trend continued for the final 2 months of school, with nearly all the pupils inventing really good games (such as Even Dominoes) and becoming adept at increasingly more difficult ones. The Spinner Game, a hard game, became a favorite of those who preferred a challenge. A memory I cherish is one of a visiting college math student playing the Spinner Game with three of my students. Because the children could add much faster than the adult, and because the visitor was amazed at their speed, the children rolled on the floor with laughter. Whenever visitors entered the room, the class liked to challenge them at addition problems. When an adult said, "I need paper and pencil to figure that out," one child had a crisp response: "We don't." Another child's response was, "That's the old-fashioned way."

THE THIRD AND FOURTH YEARS

The third and fourth years of teaching math without a textbook gave similar, positive results. Each class displayed a love of math that I had not seen during my first decade of teaching. A technique that I began to use frequently during the third year was invitational teaching. Since not all children are interested in the same thing at the same time, I began to ask, for example, "Who would like to learn how to tell time?" or, "Who would like to stay with me to work on subtraction?" Children want to become competent when we respect their individuality and do not try to force them into a mold. I often worked with small groups, while the rest of the class played games.

Another device that I began to use was a math journal. Through the years this journal was loose paper in a pocket folder, a steno pad, or a spiral notebook. The journal gave a place for students to record game points and scores, and a place for them to explain their thinking. It also provided a place to record their mental exercises. For example, if I asked, "How many ways can you make 30?" the journal showed pages of varied ways each student invented using not only addition but also subtraction and multiplication. The journal provided a place for students to invent their own problems, too—and solutions. Since students dated their work whenever they wrote in their journal, their growth in mathematical thinking could be observed by them and their parents.

CONCLUSION

As I look back, I am somewhat amazed at and yet proud of my metamorphosis. I had never given children credit for being smart enough to invent solutions. It took a lot of extra effort as a teacher to listen to what they were trying to say, and a lot of self-control to squelch the urge to take the fast-and-easy way of imposing my adult views and methods. But there was so much that never needed to be taught, because the children invented all kinds of things that had not even occurred to me. During math, I now see excitement, enthusiasm, and concentration on the children's faces. I hear voices coming from children who are self-assured, rarely timid, and quiet only while thinking.

I find myself wondering how teachers can go on depending on workbooks and drill sheets and doing all the thinking for their students. But I also recall how skeptical and unsure I was at first of not showing the children how to solve a problem the "right" way. I now know, as can be seen in Chapter 10, that these children have developed as far as, and further than, the textbook would have taken them. I am firmly convinced that the great majority learned what no book of drills could have taught them: how to think.

CHAPTER 10

Evaluation

THE WAY WE EVALUATE a program or the progress of individual children depends on the theoretical framework within which we work. Different theories about how children learn arithmetic lead to different goals and objectives, different methods of teaching, and different methods and criteria of evaluation.

In arithmetic, a major objective of traditional instruction is to get children to learn correct *techniques* of producing right answers. In the Piagetian approach, by contrast, the objectives are conceived in terms of children's ability to *think*, that is, their ability to invent various ways of solving problems and to judge whether a procedure makes logical sense. We do not stress the correctness of the answer because if children can think, they sooner or later will get the correct answer.

Achievement tests merely tell us how many correct answers a child got (raw score) and how this raw score compares with those of the child's peers (percentile rank). The only thing that counts in standardized achievement tests is the correctness of the answer, and whether an answer or procedure makes sense to the child is irrelevant to those who believe in these tests.

Furthermore, because traditional math educators have not distinguished between logico-mathematical knowledge and social-conventional knowledge, major portions of standardized tests deal with aspects of arithmetic that are social and conventional in nature. Examples of social knowledge are the "less than" sign (<) and whether "one hundred and eighteen" is written 10018, 118, or 180. Written forms of fractions also appear in achievement tests, as well as problems involving the reading of an analog clock and whether units of length are called kilograms or meters.

In this chapter, we will follow the sequence of goals and objectives discussed in the chapters in Part II. This chapter is thus divided into sections on autonomy, place value, multidigit addition, and word problems. We will conclude with a discussion of the evaluation of individual children's progress.

Throughout the chapter, we will compare the performance of second graders at Hall-Kent School with that of their peers in another suburban school where a traditional math program was followed with a textbook and workbook. There were two classes at Hall-Kent School (the classes in which algorithms were not taught) and two classes in the comparison school. The two groups will hereafter be referred to as the constructivist group ($n = 46$) and the traditional group ($n = 41$). The tables presented do not always include the same numbers of children because some were absent at the time the test was given.

The data were collected in April and May 1988, and came from the following sources:

1. The Stanford Achievement Test (SAT) mandated by the state—raw scores on three subscales (or clusters) called Place Value, Addition with Whole Numbers, and Problem Solving (word problems)
2. Videotaped individual interviews in which we examined children's understanding of place value and double-column addition as well as their handling of misaligned digits in the following problem:

$$
\begin{array}{r}
4 \\
35 \\
+\ 24 \\
\hline
\end{array}
$$

3. A group test, administered to entire classes, consisting of story problems and estimation and mental-arithmetic problems. Blank spaces were provided in this test, and children had to write their own responses

In April 1988, the mean SAT Total Mathematics score was 79 (percentile score) at Hall-Kent School and "85 or above" at the comparison school. (We say "85 or above" to protect the anonymity of the comparison school.) The socioeconomic level of the comparison school was also slightly higher.

AUTONOMY

It is difficult to assess the development of autonomy, as autonomy is complex and has many aspects. One way to evaluate children's development of autonomy in a class is to ask the teacher to leave the room for 20 minutes and to observe whether the children continue to behave well. However, the only data we were able to collect were children's responses to Question 5 of the group test, "There are 26 sheep and 10 goats on a ship.

How old is the captain?" This was a question often mentioned at math conferences to illustrate children's mindlessness resulting from traditional instruction. We had heard that many children gave the answer of 36 by adding 26 and 10.

Twenty-seven percent of the constructivist group wrote that this question did not make sense, but all the traditionally instructed children wrote "36," producing a statistically significant difference ($p < .001$). The children at Hall-Kent School were taught to be critical and to speak up when an argument did not make sense. In traditional math education, by contrast, children generally are not encouraged to think logically or to speak up when there is something they do not understand.

All the classes, both constructivist and traditional, reacted to this question with visible puzzlement and/or disturbance. When individual children raised their hands and asked questions during the test, we simply told them to think hard about the question and to put down the best answer they could. Some children at Hall-Kent School exclaimed, "It doesn't make sense!" but nevertheless wrote "36" with murmured justifications like, "He must have gotten one for each birthday."

While the difference between the two groups was statistically significant, 27% was too low. There was clearly ample room for improvement in the intellectual autonomy of the constructivist group.

PLACE VALUE

Stanford Achievement Test

The Place Value subscale of the SAT tapped mainly the social-conventional knowledge involved in place value rather than logico-mathematical knowledge. We will illustrate this point with two sample items we have made up that are similar to the actual test items. In one item, pupils were shown an expanded form such as $500 + 20 + 0$ and the following four choices: 700, 520, 50020, and 5200. This is social knowledge. The answer would be written DXX in Roman numerals. Another item showed a figure such as the example in Figure 10.1 and the following possible answers: 900, 216, 612, and 20016. Some of the children in the constructivist group had never seen place-value boxes like the one in Figure 10.1, counted the nine dots, and said that the answer was not available.

The mean raw scores for this subscale were 12.6 for the constructivist group and 14.64 for the traditional group (see Table 10.1). The maximum possible score was 15, and the difference between the two groups was not statistically significant ($p < .10$).

Figure 10.1. A figure typical of those shown in the SAT to assess children's knowledge of place value.

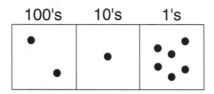

Individual Interviews

When the child came into the room for a videotaped interview, the interviewer showed him or her a 3″ × 5″ card with the numeral 16 written on it. The first request was for the child to count out "this many" from a nearby pile of chips. The interviewer then circled the 6 of 16 with the back of a pen and asked, "What does *this part* [the 6] mean? Could you show me with the chips what *this part* [the 6] means?" (No child had trouble counting out 6 chips.)

The interviewer then circled the 1 of 16 and asked, "What about *this part* [the 1]? Could you show me with the chips what *this part* [the 1] means?" (Note the use of the term *this part*, avoiding the use of any other word.) Almost all the traditionally instructed group responded by showing only one chip.

The interviewer then probed by saying, "You showed me all these chips [pointing out the 16 chips] for this number [circling the 16 on the card], and these [pointing to 6 chips] for this part [circling the 6 on the card], and this chip [pointing] for this part [circling the 1 on the card].

Table 10.1: The Constructivist and Traditional Groups' Understanding of Place Value

	Constructivist group (*n* = 46)	Traditional group (*n* = 39)	Difference	Significance
Stanford Achievement Test (mean raw score)	12.6	14.64	−2.04	.10
Explanation of the 1 in 16 (percent at Level 3)	67%	15%	52%	.001

But you didn't use any of these [pointing to the 9 or 10 chips that were not used]. Is this how it's supposed to be, or is there something strange here?" A few children replied that something was strange, but most of them said that they did not see anything wrong with their responses

The children's responses were categorized into the following three levels:

Level 1. The child showed 1 chip for the 1 in 16 and did not change his or her mind throughout the interview.

Level 2. The child at first showed 1 chip for the 1 in 16 but changed his or her mind when questioned, and ended up showing 10 chips.

Level 3. The child immediately showed 10 chips for the 1 in 16.

As can be seen in Table 10.1, 67% of the children in the constructivist group were found to be at Level 3, while only 15% of the traditionally instructed second graders were. The difference of 52 percentage points between the two groups was statistically significant ($p < .001$).

Comparison of Findings from SAT and Interviews

Two points can be made about these findings. The first is that there is a vast difference between the information provided by the SAT and by our interviews (see Table 10.1). The traditionally instructed group did very well on the SAT, coming out slightly better than the constructivist group. In our interviews, however, only 15% of the traditional group was found to understand the meaning of the 1 in 16. The results of the two methods of evaluation are in marked contradiction.

These contradictory findings are due to the fact that the SAT tapped mostly social knowledge, while our interviews tapped the logico-mathematical knowledge children represent to themselves. (Refer to Chapters 1 and 2 for a clarification of this statement.) Teachers who follow traditional methods of instruction are usually shocked when they watch their children during a live interview or on a videotape afterward. The validity of "scientific" data thus depends on the validity of the theory used. Old science gives us old, outdated data. (Refer to Chapter 1 for a clarification of this statement.)

The second point to be made is that if children do not understand place value, they cannot be expected to have number sense or to understand multidigit addition (or any other operation with numbers greater than 10). This is the topic to which we now turn.

MULTIDIGIT ADDITION

Getting Correct Answers (Stanford Achievement Test)

The most specific information obtainable from the SAT was cluster (or subscale) scores, since results from item analyses were not available. The cluster that came closest to showing children's understanding of multidigit addition was Addition with Whole Numbers. This cluster consisted of 16 computational problems, some of which involved regrouping.

As can be seen in Table 10.2, the mean raw scores of the constructivist and traditional groups were about the same on this cluster: 14.76 for the constructivist group and 15.12 for the traditional group. The maximum possible score was 16. These scores represent numbers of correct answers, and the SAT makes no attempt to find out whether children understand *why* an answer is correct.

Explaining Procedures (Individual Interviews)

For this part of the interview, the card and 16 chips used in the place-value task were left on the table, and the child was shown a 4″ × 6″ card on which the following problem was written:

$$\begin{array}{r} 16 \\ +\ 17 \\ \hline \end{array}$$

The interviewer asked the child to add these numbers mentally and to write the answer. Almost all the children in both groups gave the correct answer of 33. All the traditionally instructed children added the 6 and the 7 first and used the algorithm of "carrying." By contrast, almost all the children in the constructivist group added the tens first and then the ones, as described in Chapters 2 and 6.

The interviewer then asked the child to count out 17 chips for the second addend and to explain with the two groups of chips how he or she got the answer. The children's responses were categorized into the following three levels:

> *Level 1*. The child could not explain regrouping with chips. The children in this category showed their confusion in a surprisingly wide variety of ways, but a common attempt was: "I take 6 from 16, and 7 from 17, and that makes 13. Then I take 1 from the 13 and 1 and 1 and 1 [taken from one of the piles of 10] is 3." The interviewer probed, "I don't see 33 anywhere, and I don't understand

Table 10.2: The Constructivist and Traditional Groups' Understanding of Multidigit Addition

	Constructivist group (n = 46)	Traditional group (n = 39)	Difference	Significance
Stanford Achievement Test (mean raw score)	14.76	15.12		
Explanation of 16 +17 33	83%	23%	60%	.001
Handling of misaligned digits 4 35 +24 99	11%	79%	68%	.001

how you got 33 with what you have shown me." Some children then put out two sets of 3 chips at the bottom of the arrangement (ooo ooo) to show 33.

Level 2. The child could not explain regrouping with chips on his or her own but succeeded later as a result of the interviewer's probe as just explained.

Level 3. The child explained regrouping on his or her own with perfect logic. The traditionally instructed children at this level started with 6 + 7 and made a pile of 13 chips. They then took 10 out of the 13 and put them together with the two other heaps of 10. The children in the constructivist group, on the other hand, started with 10 + 10, often showed that 7 + 3 made another 10, and that there were thus 30 and 3.

It can be seen in Table 10.2 that 83% of the constructivist group and 23% of the traditional group were able to explain regrouping using chips, producing a statistically significant difference ($p < .001$).

Dealing with Misaligned Digits (Individual Interviews)

In the final part of the interview, we handed the child a sheet of paper on which the following misaligned problem appeared:

$$\begin{array}{r} 4 \\ 35 \\ + 24 \\ \hline \end{array}$$

Following Labinowicz (1985, p. 32), whose technique we adapted, the interviewer asked the child to "read these numbers" and then to write the answer. When the child finished, the interviewer asked him or her to read the answer aloud and then inquired, "Does that sound right?"

The proportion who wrote "99" by mechanically following the rule of adding the columns was 11% for the constructivist group and 79% for the traditionally instructed group (see Table 10.2). The difference of 68 percentage points was significant at the .001 level.

Estimation (Our Group Test)

Our group test included four problems in estimation that were presented for 4.5 seconds with an overhead projector. Since none of the second graders had had any experience estimating, we explained what was meant by estimation and gave two practice items. After asking volunteers to say what their estimates were, we encouraged children to exchange ideas about different ways in which they had thought to arrive at a reasonable estimate. When the children understood the task, we demonstrated that they would have only 4.5 seconds to look at the problem and 4.5 seconds to write the answer. The specific problems can be seen in Table 10.3. Only the first problem, 98 + 43, was given in multiple-choice format.

It can be seen in Table 10.3 that the constructivist group did better than the traditional group on all the estimation items, and that the differences were statistically significant most of the time. These findings are not surprising, since our children added the tens first when there were two digits, and the hundreds first when there were three digits. No one in the traditional group produced the correct answers to 347 + 282 and 4 × 27 within 4.5 seconds, but 7% (3 children) and 10% (4 children), respectively, of the constructivist group did. Some of our second graders can indeed add multidigit numbers faster than most adults.

Mental Arithmetic (Our Group Test)

For the mental-arithmetic part of our group test, we also used the overhead projector but increased the exposure time to 9 seconds. As can be seen in Table 10.3, significantly higher percentages of the constructivist group than of the traditional group wrote correct answers to all three of the mental-arithmetic problems—98 + 43, 3 × 31, and 4 × 27. These findings were not surprising in view of the fact that the children in the constructivist group hardly ever wrote anything in class and, instead, reflected and exchanged ideas about their thinking.

Table 10.3: The Constructivist and Traditional Groups' Estimation and Mental Arithmetic (percentage choosing or writing reasonable estimates or correct answers)

	Constructivist group (n = 42)	Traditional group (n = 41)	Difference	Significance
Estimation				
98 + 43				
Chose "about 140" [a]	69	46	23	.02
347 + 282				
Wrote number in 500–700 range	64	39	25	.01
Wrote "629"	7	0	7	.05
4 x 27				
Wrote number in 80–110 range	48	32	16	n.s.
Wrote "108"	10	0	10	.02
$3.49 + $2.75				
Wrote number in $5–$7 range	71	61	10	n.s.
Mental arithmetic				
98 + 43	48	17	31	.002
3 x 31 (31 + 31 + 31)	60 [b]	17	43	.001
4 x 27 (27 + 27 = 54, 54 + 54 = 108)	29	5	24	.002

[a] The choices were "about 110," "about 140," "about 170," and "I have no idea."

[b] Without using pencils, the constructivist second graders did better than the third graders in the fourth NAEP assessment who used pencils. In the fourth NAEP assessment, 56% of the third graders gave the correct answer (Kouba et al., 1988, p. 15).

Comparison of Findings from SAT, Interviews, and Group Test

On the Stanford Achievement Test, the traditionally instructed group and the constructivist group came out looking about the same. However, our interviews and group test revealed that the constructivist group was far superior in explaining regrouping, handling misaligned digits, and estimating sums, as well as in mental arithmetic. The total absence of items tapping children's understanding, number sense, and ability to calculate mentally is a serious flaw of the SAT. The contradictory findings again demonstrate that different theories lead to different methods and criteria of evaluation.

WORD PROBLEMS

Stanford Achievement Test

The SAT had a cluster called Problem Solving that involved word problems. As can be seen in Table 10.4, the mean raw scores on Problem Solving were almost identical for the two groups—12.62 for the constructivist group and 12.76 for the traditional group. The maximum possible score was 15.

Table 10.4: Performance of Second Graders in the Constructivist and Traditional Groups and of Third Graders in NAEP Assessment on Word Problems (percent)

| | | Grade 2 | | | |
| | | Constructivist group ($n = 41$) | Traditional group ($n = 41$) | | |
	Grade 3			Difference	Significance
Stanford Achievement Test (raw score)		12.62	12.76		
Our group test					
1. 10 cars		*61*	*29*	*32*	.002
2. 65 cents	*58*	*93*	*83*	*10*	n.s.
3. 28 children	*56*	*61*	*51*	*10*	n.s.
4. 6 cents	*29*	*56*	*29*	*27*	.007
59 − 35 = 24 cents		5	24	−19	.01
35 − 59		0	7	7	.05
. . .					
6. 92 cookies		*61*	*49*	*12*	n.s.
Correct logic		78	54	24	.02
4 + 23 = 27		5	17	−12	.05
7. 294 labels		*20*	*2*	*18*	.004
Correct logic		83	29	54	.001
21 + 14 = 35		10	29	19	.02
8. $2.40	*59*	*37*	*15*	*22*	.02
Gobstoppers: 50 cents		44	29	15	n.s.
Lifesavers: 90 cents		51	34	17	n.s.
Tootsie Pops: $1		44	29	15	n.s.

Notes: Percentages referring to correct answers are in italics. Third-grade data are from the fourth NAEP assessment (Kouba et al., 1988). For question 5, see the "Autonomy" section in this chapter.

Our Group Test

The word-problem part of our group test consisted of eight problems. They were given first, before the parts involving estimation and mental arithmetic, because some children become upset by timed tests.

The eight questions were formulated mostly on the basis of findings from the National Assessment of Educational Progress (NAEP) because of the norms it provided about third graders. Question 1 was adapted from the third NAEP assessment (Lindquist, Carpenter, Silver, & Matthews, 1983). Questions 2–4, 6, and 8 were derived from the fourth NAEP assessment (Kouba et al., 1988). Question 5, as noted earlier, had made the rounds of math conferences, and question 7 was our own creation.

In this group test, each question was read aloud while the children silently read it in their booklets. We avoided the multiple-choice format because we wanted to know the ideas that came out of the children's heads as well as their process of thinking. Below each question was a space designated for the answer and ample room to write whatever children needed to write to figure out the answer. Most of the children had plenty of time to complete each answer because we waited for almost all the children to finish answering each question.

The first column of percentages in Table 10.4 gives the findings about third graders from the fourth NAEP assessment (Kouba et al., 1988). It can be seen that the second graders in the constructivist group did better than the third graders on three of the four items for which national norms were available. The traditionally instructed second graders in our sample did as well as or better than the third graders on two of the items and less well on the other two. Let us discuss the findings from each of the questions.

Question 1. There are 49 children who want to go to the zoo. Some of their parents are willing to drive their cars and can take five children in each car. How many cars will be needed to take all 49 children to the zoo?

This is a division problem, which many second graders tackled with repeated addition. Twice as many children in the constructivist group (61%) gave the correct answer of 10 cars as in the traditional group (29%), and the difference between the two groups was significant ($p < .002$).

Only 10% in each group said that 9 cars would be needed. No one wrote "9 R 4" (because none of the second graders had received traditional instruction in division).

Question 2. At the store, a package of filler paper costs 30 cents, a roll of tape costs 35 cents, and a set of erasers costs 20 cents. What is the cost of a roll of tape and a package of filler paper? This question was similar to the following item from the fourth NAEP assessment: "At the store, a package of screws costs 30 cents, a roll of tape costs 35 cents, and a box of nails costs 20 cents. What is the cost of a roll of tape and a package of screws?" (Kouba et al., 1988, p. 18).

This question turned out to be very easy for both groups, and 93% and 83%, respectively, of the two groups gave the correct answer of 65 cents. Both of our samples of second graders did better than the third graders sampled by NAEP. The proportion who answered 85 cents (30 + 35 + 20) was 5% for the constructivist group and 12% for the traditional group.

Question 3. There were 31 children in the class at the beginning of the year. Six moved away but 3 moved into town and are new in the class. How many children are in the class now? This question was adapted from a NAEP question: "There are 31 birds on a fence. Six take off and 3 more land. How many birds are on the fence then?" (Kouba et al., 1988, p. 18).

This question involved the addition and subtraction of small numbers and yielded only a small difference between our two samples (61% for the constructivist group and 51% for the traditional group). Both of our samples of second graders did about as well as the third graders sampled by NAEP.

Question 4. Chris buys a Coke for 35 cents and French fries for 59 cents. How much change does she get back from a dollar? This question was adapted from the following question in the fourth NAEP assessment: "Chris buys a pencil for 35 cents and a soda for 59 cents. How much change does she get back from $1.00?" (Kouba et al., 1988, p. 18).

Fifty-six percent of the constructivist group and 29% of the traditional group answered this question correctly, and the difference between the two groups was significant ($p < .007$).

A surprising number in the traditionally instructed group (24%) gave the answer of 24 cents by subtracting 35 from 59. An additional 7% of the traditional group wrote "35 – 59" vertically and answers of 86, 16, and 76. These errors are errors in logic, and the constructivist group was found to be significantly better in logic.

Question 5. Since this question has already been discussed in this chapter in the section on autonomy, the results will not be reported here.

Question 6. The teacher brought 4 boxes of cookies. There are 23 cookies in each box. How many cookies are there to share all together?

The difference between the two groups (61% vs. 49%) was not significant when the proportions getting the correct answer were compared. However, when these proportions were enlarged to percentages showing correct logic (78% vs. 54%), the difference turned out to be significant ($p < .02$). An example of evidence of correct logic is a response such as "23 + 23 + 23 + 23 = 52," where the logic was correct but the answer was not.

A fairly frequent error in logic was "4 + 23 = 27," which was found among 17% of the traditional group and 5% of the constructivist group. The difference between the two groups was significant at the .05 level.

Question 7. There are 21 children in the class. If they each bring 14 soup labels, how many labels will there be all together?

This question was the hardest of the eight questions for both groups. The correct answer of 294 was given by 20% of the constructivist group and 2% of the traditional group, who all used repeated addition. The difference between the two groups was significant ($p < .004$). When the percentages demonstrating correct logic were compared (83% vs. 29%), the constructivist group again was found to have done significantly better ($p < .001$). An example of a demonstration of correct logic was to write "21" fourteen times (approximately) or "14" twenty-one times (approximately). The difference of 54 percentage points between the two groups is the largest difference in Table 10.4.

The answer of 35 (obtained by adding 21 children and 14 labels) was found among 10% of the constructivist group and 29% of the traditional group. The difference in logical thinking between the two groups was significant ($p < .02$).

Question 8. Pete bought 6 candy Gobstoppers, 3 rolls of Lifesavers, and 8 Tootsie Pops. How much did Pete spend?

Gobstoppers	Lifesavers	Tootsie Pops
3 for 25 cents	1 roll for 30 cents	4 for 50 cents

This question, too, turned out to be difficult. The correct answer of $2.40 was obtained by 37% of the constructivist group and 15% of the traditional group. The difference of 22 percentage points between the two groups was significant ($p < .02$).

The percentages who wrote correct answers for parts of the question (50 cents for Gobstoppers, 90 cents for Lifesavers, and $1.00 for Tootsie Pops) were higher in the constructivist group, but the differences were not significant.

Comparison of Findings from SAT and Group Test

Our word problems were a far cry from those of the Stanford Achievement Test. The problems on the latter were too easy, as can be seen in the following example: Johnny bought 14 oranges and gave 5 of them to Suzie. How many does he have left? Another type of problem on the SAT tapped the child's social knowledge, such as: Suzie had 4 stickers. She got 9 more. Which number sentence can you use to find how many stickers she has all together?

$$\text{(a) } 9 - 4 = \underline{\qquad} \qquad \text{(b) } 4 + 9 = \underline{\qquad} \qquad \text{(c) } \underline{\qquad} + 4 = 9$$

The easy problems on the SAT and the resultant low ceiling explain why the constructivist group looked no different from the traditional group on the SAT.

Our group test revealed that the two groups did not look different when the question was easy (e.g., Questions 2 and 3, which required only simple addition and subtraction). The differences between the two groups emerged when a question involved "division" (Question 1), "multiplication" (Questions 6 and 7), or "division," "multiplication," and addition (Question 8). The traditionally instructed group made not only numerical errors but also errors in logic. To solve word problems, children have to *logicize* each situation to know whether to add or subtract before *arithmetizing* it with precise numbers.

Achievement tests give no useful information to teachers because a raw score or percentile rank does not let them know why children selected correct or incorrect answers. Only when the child has to write on a clean sheet of paper can the teacher get some idea about the child's thinking. With our group test, however, it was possible to know that the logic of addition and subtraction was easy for the traditional group but not the logic of multiplication and division. These word problems, too, illustrate the statement we made earlier that different theories lead to different methods and criteria of evaluation.

EVALUATING INDIVIDUAL CHILDREN'S PROGRESS

We have been discussing the evaluation of an instructional program, but it is also necessary to evaluate individual children's progress. For this purpose, too, achievement tests are singularly uninformative. Since individual children's progress must be assessed over time, we have to assess what they knew and did not know at one time and compare this knowledge with what they knew and did not know at a subsequent time.

Table 10.5 shows part of an evaluation of children's progress in mental arithmetic conducted in Linda Joseph's class. This interview consisted of computational problems of various kinds. The child was given a sheet of paper on which these problems appeared in a column, on the lefthand side. The child was asked to answer the first question and to slide a ruler down to the next question. The interviewer had the same form and wrote the child's responses down and asked questions when necessary.

The 10 children listed across the top of Table 10.5 were chosen to represent both extremes of performance in the class, as well as the middle. Each child is represented once in September and again in April/May of the same school year. The plus signs in the body of the table represent the occasions when the children gave correct answers to the various problems on the test, under the conditions specified.

The last column of Table 10.5 labeled "Class %" shows the percentage of the entire class who passed each item in April/May. These percentages can be very useful to teachers when they set goals for the year. We can see from this column that double-column subtraction involving regrouping was harder for these children than some multiplication problems.

The plus signs on the first two pages of Table 10.5 represent the correct answers each child gave within 5 seconds to single-digit addition and subtraction problems. The purpose of this part of the assessment was to find out about the child's construction of the network of numerical relationships discussed in Chapter 5.

It can be seen from this part of the interview that Child 1, the one who performed the best in the spring, already had an elaborate network of numerical relationships at the beginning of the year. By contrast, Child 10, the one who was last in the rank order at the end of the year, was also the least advanced child in September. While Child 10 did not perform well at the end of the year, she did make considerable progress over the year. Although she still could not use any doubles (such as 3 + 3) in problems such as 3 + 4 in the spring, she seemed by that time to have constructed all the doubles themselves. She also showed evidence of beginning to use combinations that make 10. For example, she seems to have changed problems such as 8 + 4 to (8 + 2) + 2.

Data on the third and fourth pages of Table 10.5 concern multidigit addition, subtraction, and multiplication. There was no time limit for inclusion of correct answers in this part, and the plus signs represent correct answers arrived at in whatever way the child could. Some children counted up or down to do 13 + 8 and 27 − 8.

It can be seen in Table 10.5 that Child 1 could do almost everything on this part of the test at the beginning of the school year. The only thing with which he had trouble in September was subtraction involving re-

Table 10.5: Individual Children's Performance in Mental Arithmetic

Test Problems	September										April/May										Class %
	Child 1	Child 2	Child 3	Child 4	Child 5	Child 6	Child 7	Child 8	Child 9	Child 10	Child 1	Child 2	Child 3	Child 4	Child 5	Child 6	Child 7	Child 8	Child 9	Child 10	
Addition, 1 digit																					
Doubles																					
4 + 4	+	+		+	+	+	+	+	+	+	+	+	+	+	+	+	+	+	+	+	100
6 + 6		+	+	+		+	+	+	+		+	+	+	+		+	+	+	+	+	96
9 + 9	+	+	+	+	+		+	+			+	+	+	+	+			+	+	+	87
8 + 8	+		+	+				+		+	+	+	+	+	+	+	+	+	+	+	96
7 + 7	+	+	+	+		+			+		+	+	+	+	+	+	+	+	+	+	92
10 combos																					
8 + 2	+	+	+	+	+	+	+	+	+	+	+	+	+	+	+	+	+	+	+	+	96
3 + 7	+	+	+	+	+	+	+	+			+	+	+	+	+	+	+	+	+	+	96
4 + 6	+	+	+	+		+	+	+	+		+	+	+	+	+	+	+	+	+		83
+2																					
2 + 6	+	+	+	+	+	+	+	+	+		+	+	+	+	+	+	+	+			87
Others																					
5 + 3	+	+	+	+	+	+	+	+			+	+	+	+	+	+	+	+	+	+	83

172

Using doubles

Combination	Score
3 + 4	87
4 + 5	75
5 + 6	83
5 + 7	66
7 + 8	66

Using 10 combos

Combination	Score
7 + 4	79
8 + 4	87
9 + 4	96
8 + 5	83
9 + 7	79

3 or more addends

Combination	Score
4 + 1 + 6	75
4 + 3 + 5	58
5 + 2 + 8	58
6 / 3 / 7 / +2	33

Subtraction, 1 digit

Inverse of double

Combination	Score
12 − 6	75

(continued)

Table 10.5 (*continued*)

Test Problems	September										April/May										
	Child 1	Child 2	Child 3	Child 4	Child 5	Child 6	Child 7	Child 8	Child 9	Child 10	Child 1	Child 2	Child 3	Child 4	Child 5	Child 6	Child 7	Child 8	Child 9	Child 10	Class %
Subtraction, 1 digit (*continued*)																					
Inverse of 10 combos																					
10 − 8	+	+	+	+				+			+	+	+	+	+	+		+			83
10 − 6	+	+	+	+							+	+	+	+	+	+	+	+			83
Inverse of +2																					
7 − 2	+	+	+	+	+		+		+	+	+	+	+	+	+	+	+	+	+	+	87
Addition, 2 or more digits																					
22 +7	+	+	+	+			+		+		+	+	+	+	+	+	+	+	+	+	92
28 +31	+	+	+	+				+	+		+	+	+	+	+	+	+	+		+	96
13 +8	+	+	+	+		+	+		+		+	+	+	+	+	+	+	+	+	+	92
27 +13	+	+		+								+	+	+	+	+	+			+	75
27 + 82	+	+	+	+				+			+	+	+	+	+	+	+	+			83

174

$$\begin{array}{rr}
28 \\
+72 & 71
\end{array}$$

$$\begin{array}{rr}
254 \\
+363 & 50
\end{array}$$

$$\begin{array}{rr}
448 \\
+274 & 46
\end{array}$$

$$\begin{array}{rr}
7 \\
52 \\
+186 & 42
\end{array}$$

$$7 + 52 + 186 \qquad 33$$

Subtraction, 2 digits

$$\begin{array}{rr}
48 \\
-27 & 79
\end{array}$$

$$\begin{array}{rr}
27 \\
-8 & 62
\end{array}$$

$$\begin{array}{rr}
63 \\
-24 & 62
\end{array}$$

Multiplication

$$3 \times 7 \qquad 79$$

$$4 \times 10 \qquad 71$$

$$\begin{array}{rr}
3 \\
\times 4 & 87
\end{array}$$

$$\begin{array}{rr}
10 \\
\times 4 & 71
\end{array}$$

grouping. Although this table may give the impression that Child 1 did not learn much in second grade, his progress was made in speed and in performing operations with three- and four-digit numbers. This was one of the children who got exact, correct answers to 347 + 282 and 4 × 27 in 4.5 seconds in the estimation test.

Trailing close behind Child 1 on this part in September were Children 2 and 4. Child 2 passed all the items on this part in the spring. Child 3 actually ranked with the most advanced children, but this was "a bad day" for this child.

At the end of the rank order were Children 9 and 10. Throughout the year, these children were not able to construct place value, and this was the reason for their low performance. Child 9 often coped by drawing sticks. His performance on a task with misaligned numbers is reproduced in Figure 10.2. He drew a line to indicate 24 and drew 11 more sticks to represent 35. He then went back to the first 24 sticks and used them to count-on from 35. Then he used his fingers to add 4 more and got the answer of 62. While his answer is off by one, this is a much more intelligent procedure than mechanically adding misaligned columns and writing "99." Incidentally, Child 10, who had been taught algorithms at home, wrote "499" as the answer to the problem with misaligned columns.

Child 5 "blossomed" during the year, as can be seen in Table 10.5, especially in the second part. Her column for the second part was a total blank in September, but it was full of plus marks in April/May. We find children like her every year who show growth in spurts.

Children 6, 7, and 8 made average progress. In April/May, they comfortably added two-digit numbers involving regrouping, but three-digit

Figure 10.2. The tool invented by a child to add two-digit numbers without a system of tens.

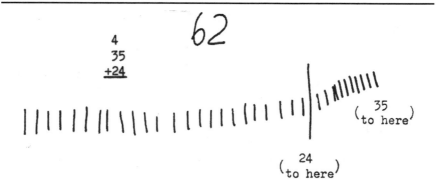

numbers were too hard for them. They also had trouble with subtraction involving regrouping.

This kind of evaluation seems much more informative to parents, teachers, and researchers than the statement that in April, Child 10 was at the 25th percentile on Total Mathematics or on a content cluster of the SAT.

CONCLUSION

We would like to conclude with a word about achievement testing and accountability. Traditional, empiricist educators assume that the job of the teacher is to put knowledge into children's heads. They also assume that the proof of this transmission is a high score on a standardized achievement test. Both of these assumptions, as we believe this book has demonstrated, are erroneous and outdated.

Piaget proved scientifically, through more than half a century of research, that children construct logico-mathematical knowledge from within. All that the teacher can do is to stimulate the child's own construction of this knowledge from the inside, as described in this book. Children come to school with the intelligence given by their families, who supply both the heredity and the environment that explain intelligence.

It is much easier for teachers to give model procedures for children to imitate than to encourage them to invent their own solutions. We have seen in this chapter and in Chapter 2, however, that the imposition of adult algorithms serves only to reinforce children's heteronomy and to hinder the development of their natural ability to think. Child 9 in Table 10.5 *will* construct place value and double-column addition, probably in third grade, if encouraged to do his own thinking.

What education needs is not higher test scores but a fundamental reexamination of our goals and objectives, and of the ways in which we try to attain these goals. If we really want independent, creative adults who can think logically and have initiative, confidence, and moral autonomy, we must seriously foster these qualities from the beginning of children's lives.

Appendix

COMMERCIALLY MADE GAMES

Addition and Subtraction Shapes (Listed in Nasco and Didax catalogs)

The Allowance Game. Carson, CA: Lakeshore Curriculum Materials, 1984. (Listed in Toys to Grow on catalog. Other versions exist but may be for older children.)

Coin Dice (Cubes) (Listed in Nasco and ETA/Cuisenaire catalogs)

Dice with many sides (Listed in Nasco, ETA/Cuisenaire, and Didax catalogs)

Flinch cards. Beverly, MA: Parker Brothers (Division of Kenner Parker Toys), 1988. Also Pawtucket, RI: Hasbro, 1998. (Distributed by Winning Moves, wmoves@cove.com)

Fudge. Ellijay, GA: Old Fashioned Crafts, 1991. (Listed in Nasco catalog)

Hundred Number Board and Hundred Number Tiles (Listed in Nasco, ETA/ Cuisenaire, and Didax catalogs)

Knock-Out. Ellijay, GA: Old Fashioned Crafts, 1992. (Listed in Nasco catalog)

Ring Toss. (Listed in S&S catalog)

Rook cards. Salem, MA: Parker Brothers, 1972. (Available in discount stores. Also distributed by Winning Moves, wmoves@cove.com)

Roulette. (Sometimes appears in Hearth Song catalog)

Safety Darts (Listed in Hearth Song catalog)

Shoot the Moon (Not available in catalog but available by calling S&S)

Shut the Box (Listed in Nasco and S&S catalogs)

Tens and Twenties. (Sometimes listed in Nasco and Didax catalogs)

Tri-Ominos (Listed in Nasco and ETA/Cuisenaire catalogs)

24 Games (Listed in Nasco and ETA/Cuisenaire catalogs)

COMPANIES WITH MAIL-ORDER CATALOGS AND/OR WEBSITES

Didax, 800-458-0024, www.didaxinc.com
ETA/Cuisenaire, 800-445-5985, www.etacuisenaire.com
Hearth Song, 800-325-2502, www.hearthsong.com
Nasco, 800-558-9595, info@eNASCO.com, modesto@eNASCO.com
S&S, 800-243-9232, www.ssww.com
Toys To Grow On, 800-542-8338, www.ttgo.com

References

Abbott, B., Faren, C., Gillham, M., Jenkins, M., Keith, A., North, M., & Pressentin, S. (1998). *CGI mathematics: Classroom action research, 1997–98.* Madison, WI: Madison Metropolitan School District.

Adjei, K. (1977). Influence of specific maternal occupation and behavior on Piagetian cognitive development. In P. R. Dasen (Ed.), *Piagetian psychology: Cross-cultural contributions* (pp. 227–256). New York: Gardner Press.

Ashlock, R. B. (1986). *Error patterns in computation.* Columbus, OH: Merrill. (Earlier editions published in 1972, 1976, and 1982)

Bovet, M. (1974). Cognitive processes among illiterate children and adults. In J. W. Berry & P. R. Dasen (Eds.), *Culture and cognition: Readings in cross-cultural psychology* (pp. 311–334). London: Methuen.

Brown, J. S., & Burton, R. R. (1978). Diagnostic models for procedural bugs in basic mathematical skills. *Cognitive Science, 2,* 155–192.

Carpenter, T. P., Ansell, E., Franke, M. L., Fennema, E., & Weisbeck, L. (1993). Models of problem solving: A study of kindergarten children's problem-solving processes, *Journal for Research in Mathematics Education, 24*(5), 428–441.

Carpenter, T. P., Fennema, E., Franke, M. L., Levi, L., & Empson, S. B. (1999). *Children's mathematics: Cognitively Guided Instruction.* Portsmouth, NH: Heinemann.

Carraher, T. N., Carraher, D. W., & Schliemann, A. D. (1985). Mathematics in the streets and in schools. *British Journal of Developmental Psychology, 3,* 21–29.

Carraher, T. N., & Schliemann, A. D. (1985). Computation routines prescribed by schools: Help or hindrance? *Journal for Research in Mathematics Education, 16,* 211–215.

Cauley, K. M. (1988). Construction of logical knowledge: Study of borrowing in subtraction. *Journal of Educational Psychology, 80,* 202–205.

Clark, F. B., & Kamii, C. (1996). Identification of multiplicative thinking in children in grades 1–5. *Journal for Research in Mathematics Education, 27,* 41–51.

Dasen, P. R. (1974). The influence of ecology, culture and European contact on cognitive development in Australian Aborigines. In J. W. Berry & P. R. Dasen (Eds.), *Culture and cognition: Readings in cross-cultural psychology* (pp. 381–408). London: Methuen.

De Lemos, M. M. (1969). The development of conservation in Aboriginal children. *International Journal of Psychology, 4*(4), 255–269.

Doise, W., & Mugny, G. (1984). *The social development of the intellect.* New York: Pergamon. (Original work published 1981)

181

Economopoulos, K., & Russell, S. J. (1998). *Putting together and taking apart: Addition and subtraction* (Part of Investigations in Number, Data, and Space). White Plains, NY: Dale Seymour.

Empson, S. B. (1995). Using sharing situations to help children learn fractions. *Teaching Children Mathematics, 2,* 110–114.

Fosnot, C. T., & Dolk, M. (2001). *Young mathematicians at work: Constructing number sense, addition, and subtraction.* Portsmouth, NH: Heinemann.

Furth, H. G. (1966). *Thinking without language.* New York: Free Press.

Ginsburg, H. P., & Opper, S. (1988). *Piaget's theory of intellectual development* (3rd ed.). Englewood Cliffs, NJ: Prentice-Hall.

Hatwell, Y. (1966). *Privation sensorielle et intelligence.* Paris: Presses Universitaires de France.

Hiebert, J., Carpenter, T. P., Fennema, E., Fuson, K. C., Wearne, D., Murray, H., Olivier, A., & Human, P. (1997). *Making sense: Teaching and learning mathematics with understanding.* Portsmouth, NH: Heinemann.

Hyde, D. M. G. (1959). *An investigation of Piaget's theories of the development of the concept of number.* Unpublished doctoral dissertation, University of London.

Inhelder, B. (1968). *The diagnosis of reasoning in the mentally retarded.* New York: John Day. (Original work published 1943)

Inhelder, B., & Piaget, J. (1964). *Early growth of logic in the child.* New York: Harper & Row. (Original work published 1959)

Inhelder, B., Sinclair, H., & Bovet, M. (1974). *Learning and the development of cognition.* Cambridge, MA: Harvard University Press.

Jones, D. A. (1975). Don't just mark the answer—have a look at the method! *Mathematics in School, 4*(3), 29–31.

Kamii, C. (1985). *Young children reinvent arithmetic.* New York: Teachers College Press.

Kamii, C. (1989a). *Double-column addition: A teacher uses Piaget's theory* [videotape]. New York: Teachers College Press.

Kamii, C. (1989b) *Young children continue to reinvent arithmetic, 2nd grade.* New York: Teachers College Press.

Kamii, C. (1994). *Young children continue to reinvent arithmetic, 3rd grade.* New York: Teachers College Press.

Kamii, C. (2000). *Young children reinvent arithmetic* (2nd ed.). New York: Teachers College Press.

Kamii, C., & Clark, F. B. (2000). *First graders dividing 62 by 5* [videotape]. New York: Teachers College Press.

Kamii, C., & DeVries, R. (1993). *Physical knowledge in preschool education.* Englewood Cliffs, NJ: Prentice-Hall. (Original work published 1978)

Kamii, C., Lewis, B. A., & Kirkland, L. D. (2001). Fluency in subtraction compared with addition. *Journal of Mathematical Behavior, 20,* 33–42.

Kamii, M. (1980, May). *Place value: Children's efforts to find a correspondence between digits and numbers of objects.* Paper presented at the tenth annual symposium of the Jean Piaget Society, Philadelphia.

Kamii, M. (1982). Children's graphic representation of numerical concepts: A developmental study (Doctoral dissertation, Harvard University, 1982). *Dissertation Abstracts International, 43*, 1478A.

Kato, Y., Kamii, C., Ozaki, K., & Nagahiro, M. (2002). Young children's representations of groups of objects: The relationship between abstraction and representation. *Journal for Research in Mathematics Education, 33*, 31–45.

Kohlberg, L. (1968). Early education: A cognitive developmental view. *Child Development, 39*, 1013–1062.

Kouba, V. L., Brown, C. A., Carpenter, T. P., Lindquist, M. M., Silver, E. A., & Swafford, J. O. (1988). Results of the fourth NAEP assessment of mathematics: Number, operations, and word problems. *Arithmetic Teacher, 35*(8), 14–19.

Kuhn, T. S. (1970). *The structure of scientific revolutions*. Chicago: University of Chicago Press.

Labinowicz, E. (1985). *Learning from children: New beginnings for teaching numerical thinking*. Menlo Park, CA: Addison-Wesley.

Laurendeau-Bendavid, M. (1977). Culture, schooling, and cognitive development: A comparative study of children in French Canada and Rwanda. In P. R. Dasen (Ed.), *Piagetian psychology: Cross-cultural contributions* (pp. 123–168). New York: Gardner Press.

Lindquist, M. M., Carpenter, T. P., Silver, E. A., & Matthews, W. (1983). The third national mathematics assessment: Results and implications for elementary and middle schools. *Arithmetic Teacher, 31*(4), 14–19.

Locke, J. (1947). *Essay concerning human understanding*. Oxford: Oxford University Press. (Original work published 1690)

Ma, L. (1999). *Knowing and teaching elementary mathematics*. Mahwah, NJ: Erlbaum.

Madell, R. (1985). Children's natural processes. *Arithmetic Teacher, 32*(7), 20–22.

McNeal, B. (1995). Learning not to think in a textbook-based mathematics class. *Journal of Mathematical Behavior, 14*, 205–234.

Mohseni, N. (1966). *La comparaison des reactions aux epreuves d'intelligence en Iran et en Europe*. Unpublished thesis, University of Paris.

Narode, R., Board, J., & Davenport, L. (1993). Algorithms supplant understanding: Case studies of primary students' strategies for double-digit addition and subtraction. In J. R. Becker & B. Pence (Eds.), *Proceedings of the 15th Annual Meeting, North American Chapter of the International Group for the Psychology of Mathematics Education, I*, 154–260.

National Council of Teachers of Mathematics. (2000). *Principles and standards for school mathematics*. Reston, VA: Author.

Opper, S. (1977). Concept development in Thai urban and rural children. In P. R. Dasen (Ed.), *Piagetian psychology: Cross-cultural contributions* (pp. 89–122). New York: Gardner Press.

Pack, S. (1997). Agreement against algorithms. *Teaching Children Mathematics, 3*, 469.

Parker, R. (1993). *Mathematical power*. Portsmouth, NH: Heinemann.

Perret-Clermont, A.-N. (1980). *Social interaction and cognitive development in children*. New York: Academic Press. (Original work published 1979)

Piaget, J. (1951). *Play, dreams, and imitation in childhood*. New York: Norton. (Original work published 1945)

Piaget, J. (1965). *The moral judgment of the child*. New York: Free Press. (Original work published 1932)

Piaget, J. (1966). Need and significance of cross-cultural studies in genetic psychology. *International Journal of Psychology, 1*(1), 3–13.

Piaget, J. (1971). *Biology and knowledge*. Chicago: University of Chicago Press. (Original work published 1967)

Piaget, J. (1973). *To understand is to invent*. New York: Grossman. (Original work published 1948)

Piaget, J. (1978). *Recherches sur la généralisation*. Paris: Presses Universitaires de France.

Piaget, J. (1980a). *Experiments in contradiction*. Chicago: University of Chicago Press. (Original work published 1974)

Piaget, J. (1980b). Foreword. In C. Kamii & R. DeVries, *Group games in early education* (p. vii). Washington, DC: National Association for the Education of Young Children.

Piaget, J. (1987). *Possibility and necessity*. Minneapolis: University of Minnesota Press. (Original work published 1983)

Piaget, J., & Garcia, R. (1989). *Psychogenesis and the history of science*. New York: Columbia University Press. (Original work published 1983)

Piaget, J., & Inhelder, B. (1973). *Memory and intelligence*. New York: Basic Books. (Original work published 1968)

Piaget, J., & Szeminska, A. (1965). *The child's conception of number*. New York: Norton. (Original work published 1941)

Plunkett, S. (1979). Decomposition and all that rot. *Mathematics in School, 8*(3), 2–7.

Price-Williams, D. R. (1961). A study concerning concepts of conservation of quantities among primitive children. *Acta Psychologica, 18*, 297–305.

Resnick, L. B. (1982). Syntax and semantics in learning to subtract. In T. P. Carpenter, J. M. Moser, & T. A. Romberg (Eds.), *Addition and subtraction: A cognitive perspective* (pp. 136–155). Hillsdale, NJ: Erlbaum.

Resnick, L. B. (1983). A developmental theory of number understanding. In H. P. Ginsburg (Ed.), *The development of mathematical thinking* (pp. 110–151). New York: Academic Press.

Richardson, K. (1996, April). *Simple tasks–complex thinking: Providing appropriate mathematical experiences for children*. Talk given at the annual meeting of the National Council of Teachers of Mathematics, San Diego.

Richardson, K. (1999). *Developing number concepts (book 3): Place value, multiplication, and division*. White Plains, NY: Dale Seymour.

Ross, S. (1986, April). *The development of children's place-value numeration concepts in grades two through five*. Paper presented at the annual meeting of the American Educational Research Association, San Francisco. (ERIC Document Reproduction Service No. ED 273 482)

Shifter, D., Bastable, V., & Russell, S. J. (1999). *Developing mathematical ideas: Number and operations, Part 1. Building a system of tens*. Parsippany, NJ: Dale Seymour.

Steffe, L. (1988). Children's construction of number sequences and multiplying schemes. In J. Hiebert & M. Behr (Eds.), *Number concepts and operations in the middle grades* (Vol. 2, pp. 119–140). Reston, VA: National Council of Teachers of Mathematics.

Steffe, L. (1992). Schemes of action and operation involving composite units. *Learning and Individual Differences, 4*, 259–309.

Taylor, F. S. (1949). *A short history of science and scientific thought*. New York: Norton.

Trafton, P. R., & Thiessen, D. (1999). *Learning through problems: Number sense and computational strategies*. Portsmouth, NH: Heinemann.

Wakefield, A. P. (1998). *Early childhood number games*. Boston: Allyn and Bacon.

Yackel, E., Cobb, P., Wood, T., Wheatley, G., & Merkel, G. (1990). The importance of social interaction in children's construction of mathematical knowledge. In T. J. Cooney & C. R. Hirsch (Eds.), *Teaching and learning mathematics in the 1990s: 1990 yearbook* (pp. 12–21). Reston, VA: National Council of Teachers of Mathematics.

Index

About the Author

Constance Kamii is professor of early childhood education at the University of Alabama at Birmingham. She previously held a joint appointment in the College of Education, University of Illinois at Chicago, and in the Faculty of Psychology and Sciences of Education, University of Geneva (Switzerland). Following receipt of her Ph.D. from the University of Michigan in 1965, she studied under Jean Piaget on and off for 15 years while working closely with teachers in classrooms to develop an early childhood curriculum based on Piaget's theory.